LEVEL 2

Jacob's Ladder

Reading Comprehension Program

Grades 4–5

LEVEL 2

Jacob's Ladder
Reading Comprehension Program

Grades 4–5

(Second Edition)

Edited by:
Joyce VanTassel-Baska
Tamra Stambaugh

Center for Gifted Education,
The College of William and Mary

Contributing Authors (in alphabetical order):
Heather French
Paula Ginsburgh
Tamra Stambaugh
Joyce VanTassel-Baska

Special Acknowledgements:
Kathryn Holt

Funded by the United States Department of Education, Javits Program

Prufrock Press Inc.
Waco, Texas

Edited by Lacy Compton
Production Design by Marjorie Parker

ISBN-13: 978-1-59363-351-6
ISBN-10: 1-59363-351-3

Prufrock Press Inc.
P.O. Box 8813
Waco, TX 76714-8813
Phone: (800) 998-2208
Fax: (800) 240-0333
http://www.prufrock.com

Contents

Part I: Teachers' Guide to Jacob's Ladder Reading Comprehension Program

Introduction to *Jacob's Ladder, Level 2*

Jacob's Ladder, Level 2 is a supplemental reading program that implements targeted readings from short stories, poetry, and nonfiction sources. With this program, students engage in an inquiry process that moves from lower order to higher order thinking skills. Starting with basic literary understanding, students learn to critically analyze texts by determining implications and consequences, generalizations, main ideas, and/or creative synthesis. Suggested for students in fourth grade to enhance reading comprehension and critical thinking, *Jacob's Ladder, Level 2* tasks are organized into four skill ladders: A–D. Each ladder focuses on a different skill. Students "climb" each ladder by answering lower level questions before moving to higher level questions or rungs at the top of each ladder. Each ladder stands alone and focuses on a separate critical thinking component in reading.

Ladder A focuses on implications and consequences. By leading students through sequencing and cause and effect activities, students learn to draw implications and consequences from readings. Ladder B focuses on making generalizations. Students first learn to provide details and examples, then move to classifying and organizing those details in order to make generalizations. Ladder C focuses on themes. Students begin by identifying setting and characters and then make inferences about the literary situation. Ladder D focuses on creative synthesis by leading students through paraphrasing and summarizing activities. Table 1 provides a visual representation of the four ladders and corresponding objectives for each ladder and rung.

TABLE 1
Goals and Objectives of *Jacob's Ladder* by Ladder and Rung

Ladder A	Ladder B	Ladder C	Ladder D
A3: Consequences and Implications	**B3: Generalizations**	**C3: Theme/Concept**	**D3: Creative Synthesis**
Students will be able to predict character actions, story outcomes, and make real-world forecasts.	Students will be able to make general statements about a reading and/or an idea within the reading, using data to support their statements.	Students will be able to identify a major idea or theme common throughout the text.	Students will create something new using what they have learned from the reading and their synopses.
A2: Cause and Effect	**B2: Classifications**	**C2: Inference**	**D2: Summarizing**
Students will be able to identify and predict relationships between character behavior and story events, and their effects upon other characters or events.	Students will be able to categorize different aspects of the text or identify and sort categories from a list of topics or details.	Students will be able to use textual clues to read between the lines and make judgments about specific textual events, ideas, or character analysis.	Students will be able to provide a synopsis of text sections.
A1: Sequencing	**B1: Details**	**C1: Literary Elements**	**D1: Paraphrasing**
Students will be able to list, in order of importance or occurrence in the text, specific events or plot summaries.	Students will be able to list specific details or recall facts related to the text or generate a list of ideas about a specific topic or character.	Students will be able to identify and explain specific story elements such as character, setting, or poetic device.	Students will be able to restate lines read using their own words.

The *Jacob's Ladder* series consists of seven levels: Primary 1, Primary 2, and Levels 1–5. Levels 1–5 contain short stories, poetry, and nonfiction selections including biography, as well as at least two commensurate ladders for each selection, with the exception of Primary 1 poetry, which has one ladder per poem. *Jacob's Ladder Primary 1* and *Primary 2* differ from the rest of the series in that the majority of the short stories are Caldecott Medal or Caldecott Honor picture books. Many of the stories are intended to be read aloud for the first reading. In addition, although *Jacob's Ladder Primary 1* does contain poetry, it does not contain nonfiction selections.

Jacob's Ladder Primary 1 is recommended for gifted readers in grades K–1, *Jacob's Ladder Primary 2* is recommended for gifted readers in grades 1–2, *Jacob's Ladder Level 1* is recommended for bright students in grades 2–3, *Jacob's Ladder Level 2* is recommended for students in grades 4–5, and *Jacob's Ladder Level 3* is recommended for students in grades 5–6. *Jacob's Ladder Level 4* and *Level 5* are recommended for middle and early high school students in grades 7–9. However, teachers may find that they want to vary usage beyond the recommended levels, depending on student abilities. Evidence suggests that the curriculum can be successfully implemented with gifted learners and advanced readers, as well as promising learners, at different grade levels. Thus, the levels vary and overlap to provide opportunities for teachers to select the most appropriate set of readings for meaningful differentiation for their gifted, bright, or promising learners.

Ladder A: Focus on Implications and Consequences

The goal of Ladder A is to develop prediction and forecasting skills by encouraging students to make connections among the information provided. Starting with sequencing, students learn to recognize basic types of change that occur within a text. Through identifying cause and effect relationships, students then can judge the impact of certain events. Finally, through recognizing consequences and implications, students predict future events as logical and identify both short- and long-term consequences by judging probable outcomes based on data provided. The rungs are as follows:

- **Ladder A, Rung 1, Sequencing**: The lowest rung on the ladder, sequencing, requires students to organize a set of information in order, based on their reading (e.g., List the steps of a recipe in order).
- **Ladder A, Rung 2, Cause and Effect**: The middle rung, cause and effect, requires students to think about relationships and identify what causes certain effects and/or what effects were brought about because of certain causes (e.g., What causes a cake to rise in the oven? What effect does the addition of egg yolks have on a batter?).
- **Ladder A, Rung 3, Consequences and Implications**: The highest rung on Ladder A requires students to think about both short-term

and long-term events that may happen as a result of an effect they have identified (e.g., What are the short-term and long-term consequences of baking at home?). Students learn to draw consequences and implications from text for application in the real world.

Ladder B: Focus on Generalizations

The goal of Ladder B is to help students develop deductive reasoning skills, moving from the concrete elements in a story to abstract ideas. Students begin by learning the importance of concrete details and how they can be organized. By the top rung, students are able to make general statements spanning a topic or concept. The rungs are as follows:

- **Ladder B, Rung 1, Details**: The lowest rung on Ladder B, details/examples, requires students to list examples or details from what they have read and/or to list examples they know from the real world or have read about (e.g., Make a list of examples of transportation. Write as many as you can think of in 2 minutes).
- **Ladder B, Rung 2, Classifications**: The middle rung of Ladder B focuses on students' ability to categorize examples and details based on characteristics (e.g., How might we categorize the modes of transportation you identified?). This activity builds students' skills in categorization and classification.
- **Ladder B, Rung 3, Generalizations**: The highest rung on Ladder B, generalization, requires students to use the list and categories generated at Rungs 1 and 2 to develop 2–3 general statements that apply to *all* of their examples (e.g., Write three statements about transportation).

Ladder C: Focus on Themes

The goal of Ladder C is to develop literary analysis skills based on an understanding of literary elements. After completing Ladder C, students state main themes and ideas of text after identifying setting, characters, and the context of the piece. The rungs are as follows:

- **Ladder C, Rung 1, Literary Elements**: While working on Rung 1, students identify and/or describe the setting or situation in which the reading occurs. This rung also requires students to develop an understanding of given characters by identifying qualities he or she possesses and comparing these qualities to other characters they have encountered in their reading (e.g., In *Goldilocks and the Three Bears*, what is the situation in which Goldilocks finds herself? What qualities do you admire in Goldilocks? What qualities do you find problematic? How is she similar or different from other fairy tale characters you have encountered?).

- **Ladder C, Rung 2, Inference**: Inference serves as the middle rung of this ladder and requires students to think through a situation in the text and come to a conclusion based on the information and clues provided (e.g., What evidence exists that Goldilocks ate the porridge? What inferences can you make about the bear's subsequent action?).
- **Ladder C, Rung 3, Theme/Concept**: As the highest rung of Ladder C, this step requires students to state the central idea or theme for a reading. This exercise asks students to explain an idea from the reading that best states what the text means (e.g., How would you rename the fairy tale? Why? What is the overall theme of *Goldilocks and the Three Bears*? Which of the following morals apply to the fairy tale? Why or why not?).

Ladder D: Focus on Creative Synthesis

The goal of Ladder D is to help students develop skills in creative synthesis in order to foster students' creation of new material based on information from the reading. It moves from the level of restating ideas to creating new ideas about a topic or concept. The rungs are as follows:

- **Ladder D, Rung 1, Paraphrasing**: The lowest rung on Ladder D is paraphrasing. This rung requires students to restate a short passage using their own words (e.g., Rewrite the following quotation in your own words: "But as soon as [the slave] came near to Androcles, he recognized his friend, and fawned upon him, and licked his hands like a friendly dog. The emperor, surprised at this, summoned Androcles to him, who told the whole story. Whereupon the slave was pardoned and freed, and the Lion let loose to his native forest.").
- **Ladder D, Rung 2, Summarizing**: Summarizing, the middle rung, requires students to summarize larger sections of text by selecting the most important key points within a passage (e.g., Choose one section of the story and summarize it in five sentences).

- **Ladder D, Rung 3, Creative Synthesis**: The highest rung on Ladder D requires students to create something new using what they have learned from the reading and their synopses of it (e.g., Write another fable about the main idea you identified for this fable, using characters, setting, and a plot of your choice).

Process Skills

Along with the four goals addressed by the ladders, a fifth goal, process skills, is incorporated in the *Jacob's Ladder* curriculum. The aim of this goal is to promote learning through interaction and discussion of reading material in the classroom. After completing the ladders and following guidelines for discussion and teacher feedback, students will be able to:

- articulate their understanding of a reading passage using textual support,
- engage in proper dialogue about the meaning of a selection, and
- discuss varied ideas about intention of a passage both orally and in writing.

Reading Genres and Selections

The reading selections include three major genres: short stories (fables, myths, short stories, and essays), poetry, and nonfiction. In Level 2, each reading within a genre has been carefully selected or tailored for fourth-grade reading accessibility and interest. The stories and poems for the *Jacob's Ladder* curriculum at each grade level were chosen with three basic criteria in mind: (1) concrete to abstract development, (2) level of vocabulary, and (3) age-appropriate themes. The readings and exercises are designed to move students forward in their abstract thinking processes by promoting critical and creative thinking. The vocabulary in each reading is grade-level appropriate, however when new or unfamiliar words are encountered, they should be covered in class before readings and ladder questions are assigned. Themes also are appropriate to the students' ages at each grade level and were chosen to complement themes typically seen in texts for each particular level. The short stories, poetry, and nonfiction readings with corresponding ladder sets are delineated in Part II. Table 2 outlines all Level 1 readings by genre.

TABLE 2
Reading Selections by Genre

Short Stories	Poetry	Nonfiction
Androcles	A Bedtime Story	The American Revolutionary War
Arachne and Athena	Cousin for Sale	The Exploration of Space
The Blue Heron	Grapefruit	Graphic Ice Cream
Clay Marbles, Alexei, and Me	Lift Every Voice and Sing	The Great Depression
The Fox and the Cat	My Shadow	It's Electric
The Lost Wig	My Sister Is a Sissy	The Metric System vs. The U. S. Customary Systems
Mary Poppins' Secret	Occupant of Room # 709	
The Myth of Athena	Overpopulation	
The Myth of Heracles (Hercules)	School House Is A-Rockin'	
Theseus and the Minotaur	Untitled	

Rationale

Constructing meaning of the written word is one of the earliest tasks required of students in schools. This skill occupies the central place in the curriculum at the elementary level. Yet, approaches to teaching reading comprehension often are "skill and drill," using worksheets on low-level reading material. As a result, students frequently are unable to transfer these skills from exercise pages and apply them to new higher level reading material.

The time expended to ensure that students become autonomous and advanced readers would suggest the need for a methodology that deliberately moves students from simple to complex reading skills with grade-appropriate texts. Such a learning approach to reading skill development ensures that students can traverse easily from basic comprehension skills to higher level critical reading skills, while using the same reading stimulus to navigate this transition. Reading comprehension is enhanced by instructional scaffolding, moving students from lower order to higher order thinking, using strategies and processes to help students analyze passages (Fielding & Pearson, 1994; Villaume & Brabham, 2002). In addition, teachers who emphasize higher order thinking through questions and tasks such as those at the higher rungs of each ladder promote greater reading growth (Knapp et al., 1995; Taylor, Pearson, Peterson, & Rodriguez, 2003).

Jacob's Ladder was written in response to teacher findings that students needed additional scaffolding to consistently work at higher levels of thinking in reading. In addition, an analysis of reading reform curriculum by the American Federation of Teachers (AFT, 1998) shows that only two of the recommended curricula posit a research base and a focus on critical thinking skills in reading. Similarly, Tivnan and Hemphill (2005) studied reading reform curricula in Title I schools and found that none of the reading programs studied emphasized skills beyond basic phonemic awareness, fluency, or limited comprehension. Therefore, supplementary curriculum that focuses on higher level thinking skills is needed.

The *Jacob's Ladder* program is a compilation of the instructional scaffolding and reading exercises necessary to aid students in their journey toward becoming critical readers. Students learn concept development skills through learning to generalize, predicting and forecasting skills through delineating implications of events, and literary analysis skills through discerning textual meaning. The questions and tasks for each reading are open-ended, as this type of approach to responding to literature improves performance on comprehension tests (Guthrie, Schafer, & Huang, 2001). Progressing through the hierarchy of skills also requires students to re-read the text, thereby improving metacomprehension accuracy (Rawson, Dunlosky, & Thiede, 2000).

Research Base

A quasi-experimental study was conducted using *Jacob's Ladder* as a supplementary program for students in Title I schools, grades 3–5. After professional development occurred, experimental teachers were instructed to implement the *Jacob's Ladder* curriculum in addition to their basal reading series and guided reading groups. Teachers in the control group taught their district-adopted textbook reading series as the main curriculum.

Findings from this study ($N = 495$) suggest that when compared to students who used the basal reader only, those students who were exposed to the *Jacob's Ladder* curriculum showed significant gains in reading comprehension and critical thinking. Likewise, students who used the curriculum showed significant and important growth on curriculum-based assessments that included determining implications/consequences, making inferences, outlining themes and generalizations, and applying creative synthesis. Students reported greater interest in reading and eluded that the curriculum made them "think harder." Teachers reported more in-depth student discussion and personal growth in the ability to ask open-ended questions when reading (Stambaugh, 2008).

Implementation Considerations

Teachers need to consider certain issues when implementing the *Jacob's Ladder* curriculum. Although the program is targeted for promising students who need more exposure to higher level thinking skills in reading, the program may be suitable for learners who are functioning above or below grade level.

As modeling, coaching, and feedback appear to enhance student growth in reading and writing (Pressley et al., 2001; Taylor, Peterson, Pearson, & Rodriguez, 2002), it is recommended that teachers review how to complete the task ladders with the entire class at least once, outlining expectations and record-keeping tasks, as well as modeling the process prior to assigning small-group or independent work. Students should complete the ladder tasks on their own paper or on the template provided in Appendix B. As students gain more confidence in the curriculum, the teacher should allow more independent work coupled with small group or paired discussion, and then whole-group sharing with teacher feedback.

Completing these activities in dyads or small groups will facilitate discussions that stress collaborative reasoning, thereby fostering greater engagement and higher level thinking (Chin, Anderson, & Waggoner, 2001; Pressley et al., 2001; Taylor et al., 2002). The stories and accompanying ladder questions and activities also may be organized into a reading center in the classroom or utilized with reading groups during guided reading.

Process of *Jacob's Ladder*

The process of inquiry and feedback, as led and modeled by the teacher, is critical to the success of the program and student mastery of process skills. Teachers need to encourage and solicit multiple student responses and encourage dialogue about various perspectives and interpretations of a given text, requiring students to justify their answers with textual support and concrete examples. Student use of the ladders depends on teacher stance and modeling as well as student readiness. After teacher modeling, students should understand how to use the ladders as prescribed by the teacher. Sample follow-up questions such as those listed below can be used by the teacher and posted in the classroom to help guide student discussion.

- That's interesting; does anyone have a different idea?
- What in the story makes you say that?

- What do you think the author means by . . . ?
- What do you think are the implications or consequences to . . . ?
- Did anyone view that differently? How?
- Does anyone have a different point of view? Justify your answer.
- In the story I noticed that . . . Do you think that might have significance to the overall meaning?
- I heard someone say that he thought the poem (story) was about . . . What do you think? Justify your answer from the events of the story.
- Do you notice any key words that might be significant? Why?
- Do you notice any words that give you a mental picture? Do those words have significance? What might they symbolize?
- I agree with . . . because
- I had a different idea than . . . because

Grouping Students

Jacob's Ladder may be used in a number of different grouping patterns. The program should be introduced initially as a whole-group activity directed by the teacher with appropriate open-ended questions, feedback, and monitoring. After students have examined each type of ladder with teacher guidance, they should be encouraged to use the program by writing ideas independently, sharing with a partner, and then discussing the findings with a group. The dyad approach provides maximal opportunities for student discussion of the readings and collaborative decisions about the answers to questions posed. One purpose of the program is to solicit meaningful discussion of the text. Like-ability groups are recommended (Kulik & Kulik, 1992) for discussion.

Pre- and Postassessments and Grading

The pre- and postassessments included in Appendix A were designed as a diagnostic-prescriptive approach to guide program implementation prior to the implementation of *Jacob's Ladder*. The pretest should be administered, scored, and then used to guide student instruction and the selection of readings for varied ability groups. Both the pre- and postassessment, scoring rubric, and sample exemplars for each rubric category and level are included in Appendix A along with exemplars to guide scoring.

In both the pre- and postassessments, students read a short passage and respond to the four questions. Question 1 focuses on implications and consequences (Ladder A); Question 2 on generalization, theme, and concept (Ladders B and C); Question 3 on inference (Ladder C); and Question 4 on creative synthesis (Ladder D). By analyzing each question and scored response, teachers may wish to guide reading selections toward the appropriate ladders and stories based on student need.

Upon conclusion of the program or as a midpoint check, the posttest may be administered to compare the pretest results and to measure growth in students' responses. These pre/post results could be used as part of a student portfolio, in a parent-teacher conference, or documentation of curriculum effectiveness and student progress. The pre- and postassessments were piloted to ensure that both forms were equivalent in difficulty (α = .76) and that the interrater reliability of scorers was appropriate (α = .81).

Student Reflection, Feedback, and Record Keeping

Students may use an answer sheet such as the one provided in Appendix B for each ladder to record their personal thoughts independently before discussing with a partner. After finishing both of the ladders for each reading selection, a reflection page (also in Appendix B) can be provided, indicating the student's personal assessment of the work completed. Teachers also will want to check student answers as ladder segments are completed and conduct an error analysis. Individual or small-group consultation should occur at this time to ensure that students understand what they did incorrectly and why. In order to analyze student responses and progress across the program, teachers need to monitor student performance, using the student answer sheets to indicate appropriate completion of tasks. Specific comments about student work also are important to promote growth and understanding of content.

Record-keeping sheets for the class also are provided in Appendix B. On these forms, teachers record student progress on a 3-point scale: 2 *(applies skills very effectively)*, 1 (*understands and applies skills*), or a 0 (*needs more practice with the given skill set*) across readings and ladder sets. This form can be used as part of a diagnostic-prescriptive approach to selecting reading materials and ladders based on student understanding or the need for more practice.

Sample Concluding Activities

Grading the ladders and responses are at the teacher's discretion. Teachers should not overemphasize the lower rungs in graded activities. Lower rungs are intended only as a vehicle to the higher level questions at the top of the ladder. Instead, top rung questions may be used as a journal prompt or as part of a graded open-ended writing response. Grades also could be given based on guided discussion after students are trained on appropriate ways to discuss literature. Additional ideas for grading are as follows:

- Write a persuasive essay to justify what you think the story is about.
- Create a symbol to show the meaning of the story. Write two sentences to justify your answer.
- In one word or phrase, what is this story mostly about? Justify your answer using examples from the story.
- Write a letter from the author's point of view, explaining what the meaning of the story is to young children.
- Pretend you are an illustrator. Create a drawing for the story or poem that shows the main idea or theme. Write a sentence that describes your illustration and theme.

Time Allotment

Although the time needed to complete *Jacob's Ladder* tasks will vary by student, most ladders should take students 15 minutes to read the selection and another 15–20 minutes to complete one ladder individually. More time is required for paired student and whole-group discussion of the questions. Teachers may wish to set aside 2 days each week for focusing on one *Jacob's Ladder* reading and the two commensurate ladders, especially when introducing the program.

Answer Key

An answer key is included at the end of the book. It contains a set of suggested answers for all questions related to each reading selection. All of the questions are somewhat open-ended; therefore, answers may vary. The answers provided in the key are simply suggestions to help illustrate the skills targeted by each ladder skill set.

Alignment to Standards

Tables 3, 4, and 5 contain alignment charts to demonstrate the connection of the fiction and nonfiction reading materials to relevant national standards in all subject areas. One of the benefits of this program is its ability to provide cross-disciplinary coverage of standards through the use of a single reading stimulus.

TABLE 3
Standards Alignment: Short Stories

Language Arts—Short Stories	Androcles	Athena and Arachne	The Blue Heron	Clay Marbles, Aleksei, & Me	The Fox and the Cat	The Lost Wig	Mary Poppins' Secret	The Myth of Athena	The Myth of Heracles	Theseus and the Minotaur
The student will use analysis of text, including the interaction of the text with reader's feelings and attitudes to create response.		✘				✘		✘		
The student will interpret and analyze the meaning of literary works from diverse cultures and authors by applying different critical lenses and analytic techniques.	✘	✘	✘	✘	✘	✘	✘	✘	✘	✘
The student will integrate various cues and strategies to comprehend what he or she reads.	✘	✘	✘	✘	✘	✘	✘	✘	✘	✘
The student will use knowledge of the purposes, structures, and elements of writing to analyze and interpret various types of text.	✘	✘	✘	✘	✘	✘	✘	✘	✘	✘
Students will use word-analysis skills, context clues, and other strategies to read fiction and nonfiction with fluency and accuracy.	✘	✘	✘	✘	✘	✘	✘	✘	✘	✘

TABLE 4
Standards Alignment: Poetry

Language Arts—Poetry	A Bedtime Story	Cousin for Sale	Grapefruit	Lift Every Voice	My Shadow	My Sister	Occupant of Room #709	Overpopulation	School House	Untitled
The student will use analysis of text, including the interaction of the text with reader's feelings and attitudes to create response.	✘	✘	✘	✘	✘	✘	✘	✘	✘	✘
The student will interpret and analyze the meaning of literary works from diverse cultures and authors by applying different critical lenses and analytic techniques.	✘	✘	✘	✘	✘	✘	✘		✘	✘
The student will integrate various cues and strategies to comprehend what he or she reads.	✘	✘	✘	✘	✘	✘	✘	✘		✘
The student will use knowledge of the purposes, structures, and elements of writing to analyze and interpret various types of text.	✘	✘		✘	✘	✘		✘	✘	✘
Students will use word-analysis skills, context clues, and other strategies to read fiction and nonfiction with fluency and accuracy.				✘						

Table 5
Standards Alignment: Nonfiction

Social Studies, Science, and Math Standards	The American Revolutionary War	The Exploration of Space	Graphic Ice Cream	The Great Depression	It's Electric	The Metric System vs. The U.S. Customary System
Social Studies Standards						
Culture	✗			✗		
Time, Continuity, and Change	✗			✗		
People, Places, and Environments						
Individual Development and Identity						
Individuals, Groups, and Institutions	✗			✗		
Science, Technology, and Society						
Science Standards						
Science as Inquiry		✗				
Physical Science		✗			✗	
Life Science						
Earth and Space Science		✗				
Science and Technology		✗			✗	
Science in Personal and Social Perspectives						
History and Nature of Science					✗	
Math Standards						
Number and Operations						✗
Geometry						
Measurement			✗			✗
Data Analysis and Probability			✗			
Problem Solving						
Communication						
Connections						

References

American Federation of Teachers. (1998). *Building on the best, learning from what works: Seven promising reading and English language arts programs.* Washington, DC: Author.

Chin, C. A., Anderson, R. C., & Waggoner, M. A. (2001). Patterns of discourse in two kinds of literature discussion. *Reading Research Quarterly, 36,* 378–411.

Fielding, L. G., & Pearson, P. D. (1994). Reading comprehension: What works. *Educational Leadership, 51*(5), 62–67.

Guthrie, J. T., Schafer, W. D., & Huang, C. (2001). Benefits of opportunity to read and balanced reading instruction on the NAEP. *Journal of Educational Research, 94,* 145–162.

Knapp, M. S., Adelman, N. E., Marder, C., McCollum, H., Needels, M. C., Padilla, C., et al. (1995). *Teaching for meaning in high-poverty classrooms.* New York: Teachers College Press.

Kulik, J. A., & Kulik, C. (1992). Meta-analytic findings on grouping programs. *Gifted Child Quarterly, 36,* 73–77.

Pressley, M., Wharton-McDonald, R., Allington, R., Block, C. C., Morrow, L., Tracey, D., et al. (2001). A study of effective first-grade literacy instruction. *Scientific Studies of Reading, 5,* 35–58.

Rawson, K. A., Dunlosky, J., & Thiede, K. W. (2000). The rereading effect: Metacomprehension accuracy improves across reading trials. *Memory & Cognition, 28,* 1004–1010.

Stambaugh, T. (2008). *Effects of the Jacob's Ladder Reading Comprehension Program.* Manuscript submitted for publication.

Taylor, B. M., Pearson, P. D., Peterson, D. S., & Rodriguez, M. C. (2003). Reading growth in high-poverty classrooms: The influence of teacher practices that encourage cognitive engagement in literacy learning. *The Elementary School Journal, 104,* 3–30.

Taylor, B. M., Peterson, D. S., Pearson, P. D., & Rodriguez, M. C. (2002). Looking inside classrooms: Reflecting on the "how" as well as the "what" in effective reading instruction. *Reading Teacher, 56,* 270–279.

Tivnan, T., & Hemphill, L. (2005). Comparing four literacy reform models in high-poverty schools: Patterns of first grade achievement. *Elementary School Journal, 105,* 419–443.

Villaume, S. K., & Brabham, E. G. (2002). Comprehension instruction: Beyond strategies. *The Reading Teacher, 55,* 672–676.

Part II: Readings and Student Ladder Sets

Chapter 1

Short Stories

Chapter 1 includes the selected readings and accompanying question sets for each short story selection. Each reading is followed by two sets of questions; each set is aligned to one of the four ladder skills. For *Jacob's Ladder 2,* the skills covered by each selection are as follows:

Title	Ladder Skills
Androcles	C, D
Arachne and Athena	B, C
The Blue Heron	A, B
Clay Marbles, Aleksei, and Me	B, C
The Fox and the Cat	B, C
The Lost Wig	A, C
Mary Poppins' Secret	C, D
The Myth of Athena	A, D
The Myth of Heracles	A, D
Theseus and the Minotaur	B, D

Name: ______________________________ Date: ______________

Androcles

A slave named Androcles once escaped from his master and fled to the forest. As he was wandering there he came upon a lion lying down moaning and groaning. At first he turned to flee, but finding that the lion did not pursue him, he turned back and went up to him. As he came near, the lion put out his paw, which was all swollen and bleeding, and Androcles found that a huge thorn had got into it, and was causing all the pain. He pulled out the thorn and bound up the paw of the lion, who was soon able to rise and lick the hand of Androcles like a dog. Then the lion took Androcles to his cave, and every day brought him meat for his survival. But shortly afterward both Androcles and the lion were captured, and the slave was sentenced to be thrown to the lion, after the latter had been kept without food for several days. The Emperor and all of his court came to see the spectacle, and Androcles was led out into the middle of the arena. Soon the lion was let loose from his den, and rushed bounding and roaring towards his victim. But as soon as he came near to Androcles he recognized his friend, and fawned upon him, and licked his hands like a friendly dog. The Emperor, surprised at this, summoned Androcles to him, who told him the whole story, whereupon the slave was pardoned and freed, and the lion let loose to his native forest.

Name: ____________________ Date: ____________

Theme/Concept

C3

Write a moral for the fable. Explain why your moral is appropriate, providing evidence from the text.

Inference

C2

Why doesn't the Lion eat Androcles? Did it surprise you that the Lion spared him? Why or why not?

ANDROCLES

Literary Elements

C1

How would you describe Androcles? Support your answer with evidence from the text.

Name: ____________________ Date: ____________

Creative Synthesis

D3

Write another fable about the main idea you identified for this fable, using characters, setting, and a plot of your choice.

Summarizing

D2

In a sentence, write the main idea of the fable about Androcles. Support your answer with evidence from the text.

Paraphrasing

D1

Rewrite the following quotation in your own words: "But as soon as he came near to Androcles he recognized his friend, and fawned upon him, and licked his hands like a friendly dog. The Emperor, surprised at this, summoned Androcles to him, who told him the whole story, whereupon the slave was pardoned and freed, and the Lion let loose to his native forest."

ANDROCLES

Name: ______________________________ Date: ______________

Arachne and Athena

Arachne, who lived in Greece during ancient times, was famous for her incredible talent in weaving cloth. She could make the most beautiful cloth in the entire land. However, Arachne was not a modest girl. She would walk through the city boasting about her incredible talents. Arachne would even tell people that she was better at weaving than the revered goddess Athena.

Athena was not pleased by Arachne's boasting. One day, Athena knocked on Arachne's door. Arachne opened the door to find an old lady dressed in ragged clothes. She did not know she was really looking at Athena in disguise. The old lady pretended to be interested in buying some of Arachne's cloth. Arachne let the old lady enter. Immediately, Athena, disguised as the old lady, started criticizing Arachne's weaving, saying she could do much better. Insulted, Arachne challenged the old lady to a weaving contest.

After accepting the challenge, Athena emerged from her disguise. Arachne was not at all frightened by the prospect of a weaving competition with Athena; Arachne was completely convinced she would win!

Both Arachne and Athena spent hours weaving beautiful cloth. Athena's cloth was spectacular. She had woven a picture of the gods performing their many wonderful deeds. Arachne's cloth also portrayed the gods and was equally stunning. However, Arachne's cloth portrayed the gods at their weakest moments, displaying their worst behavior. Athena was furious. She could not believe Arachne had the audacity to insult the gods.

Athena complimented Arachne on her amazing weaving talent and told her she would be justly rewarded for her gifts. Arachne felt her head begin to shrink and watched in horror as six furry legs sprouted from her body. Athena told her to enjoy spending the rest of her days weaving all she wished.

Name: ______________________ Date: ______________

ARACHNE AND ATHENA

Generalizations

B3

What generalizations can you make about change based on your list and categories?

Classifications

B2

Using the list you created in B1, categorize the changes you listed.

Details

B1

List 25 ways Arachne's life might change now that she is a spider.

Name: ______________________ Date: ______________

ARACHNE AND ATHENA

Theme/Concept

C3

What moral could we learn from this myth?
Support your answer with evidence from the text.

Inference

C2

Why did Arachne try to out-weave Athena?
What in the text makes you think so?

Literary Elements

C1

Using a Venn diagram, compare and contrast the characters Arachne and Athena.

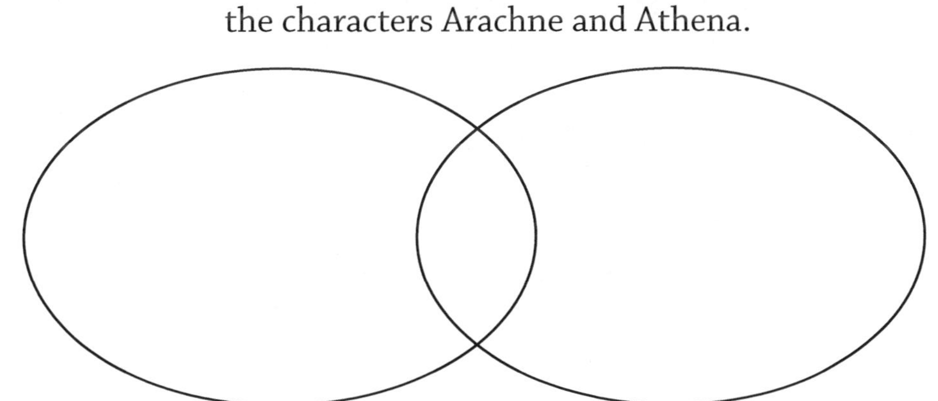

Name: ______________________ Date: ______________

The Blue Heron

As I looked through the cold April drizzle at the Great Blue Heron perched on the log, I thought, "God went all out on this one!" It was a foul day. The drizzle was cold, and everything reeked of swamp and decaying wood. I stared at the heron encircled in a wreath of Spanish moss. It was a perfect picture. I wished with all my soul that I would have a camera in my hands instead of a rifle when I looked down. It didn't happen and I was thinking of a way out of the situation, when my father interrupted my thoughts.

"Shoot, Jon!" He whispered fiercely, "It's going to fly away before you can even raise the blasted gun!"

My pa was touchy because he knew that if I let this shot slip, it would be a lot of money down the drain.

Reluctantly, I raised the sight to my eye, not wanting to spoil the view. Hesitantly, I aimed, shut my eyes tightly, and fired. I heard the shot ring out, and I prayed that God would forgive me for killing one of his creatures that is as beautiful as this. I never wanted to shoot any bird, but if I told my pa that, he would disown me.

When I looked up, it looked as if an invisible hand had swiped the heron from its perch. My pa sprang up to get the prize. He carried it back and handed it to me so he could pat me on the shoulder.

"Nice job, Jon! Clean through the eye!" The best I could give him in return was a quavery smile and a weak, "Thanks," although praise from my father came about as often as a snowstorm in a desert.

Pa didn't notice the quiver in my voice, but kept on walking, talking about how I would become an excellent hunter one day, and how much money I was going to bring the family.

As we headed home, I tried to clear my mind, but all I could see was the heron being knocked off its perch, and my pa showing me the bullet hole where the eye had once been.

I was so engrossed in wallowing in pity for the bird that I nearly walked into the cypress tree next to our house. Pa called me into the barn to help with the evening chores.

After the chores were done, Pa left me to skin the bird. It was then that I realized that the bird was a female, and it also was nesting season. Then the harsh reality hit me as hard as the bullet must have hit the heron; that poor mother had been luring us away from her nest.

I went to bed with a sick stomach and tossed and turned the entire night with guilt. The next morning it was raining so hard that I could barely find my way to the barn to do my chores. I wondered if there were any chicks in the nest. Concentrating on anything was impossible, as my mind kept wandering to the heron. I couldn't even hear, and my parents grew worried. My mother took me into the pantry and looked at my tongue, turned my eyelid inside out, and made me swallow a spoonful of bitter, black medicine. After that, she put me to bed for the rest of the day.

The next morning was beautiful, and after I had convinced my mother that I was healthy, I told her that I was going out to play. I stole some cornbread, and went to the place where I had shot the heron.

The water was about a foot higher than it had been, and I traipsed all around the swamp, finding three small chicks in it. I leaned down to see if any of them were alive. Two were dead, but the third one twitched and squeaked. It gave such a weak cry that my heart almost broke. I stooped down, crumbled the cornbread in my hand, and mixed it with swamp water, so I had a type of cornbread clabber. As gently I could, I pried open the mouth of this chick, and poured the crude mixture down its throat.

After I had forced the chick to eat, I took off my shirt and bundled the chick in it. The path home was rough, and it was a task of gargantuan proportion trying not to jolt the pitiful little thing in my arms.

Once at home, I carefully snuck the baby bird into the warmest, driest, and most remote corner of the hay loft that I could find. I lay the chick in a little nest that I scooped out, and piled some hay up next to it, so it was completely hidden. The warmth of the stock beneath it, and the sound of the horses and cows chewing their hay, and the content snorting of the pigs put it right to sleep. I decided to name it Crest.

The bird was quite safe there and for the next 4 weeks, Crest remained a secret. I snuck up to feed him 3 times a day when I was doing the chores. We quickly became friends, and he surprised me one day by stumbling around the loft, flapping his wings. This frightened me because if my pa ever came up and saw him stumbling around, there would be trouble.

In the end, I had to resort to the cruelest measure of torture by tying his feet together and pinioning his wings. I was thankful that Crest was a quiet creature.

My thankfulness didn't last long. One day, 2 months after I'd first found Crest, Pa came in from the barn after feeding the horses, carrying in a struggling Crest by his legs.

"Son?" he question me fiercely, "I heard a rustle in the hayloft, and went up there to find this!" Pa presented my bird triumphantly and shook it. My father hated any man that took pity on animals that could bring in money.

"Pa! I can explain!" I cried desperately. "He was dying! He would've died!"

Name: ________________________________ Date: ________________

"If he didn't die then, he's gonna die now!" He flung the bird on the floor and got his shotgun from against the wall. My mother ran out of the room, terrified.

"Pa! NO!" I screamed. I lunged forward and managed to dive in front of the bird milliseconds before the shot reach the animal. All of a sudden, I felt a sudden numbness in my stomach, then white fire. The room started spinning in an uncontrollable vertigo. I saw my two sisters, their faces buried in my mother's skirt; my mother, hands pressed tightly against her lips, her face white with terror. I saw my father on his knees, looking toward the heavens, screaming, and then Crest. I made a final lunge for him, and then black overcame me.

I slipped in and out of consciousness for a week. When I finally woke up, I thought, "What a terrible dream!" I tried to roll over, but I felt white fire in my stomach. I groaned in agony.

"So, it wasn't a dream?" I whispered. My vision blurred, then cleared. My mother came toward me and pressed a cool damp cloth against my forehead.

My father gently touched her on the shoulder, and she stepped aside.

"Son?" he said gruffly, "How are you?"

"I've been better." I managed a feeble laugh.

"I'm sorry." His voice cracked, "So sorry . . ." My pa's voice trailed off and he began to cry. That sight startled me, but I had to be strong now.

"It's all right," I said in a soothing voice. "Everything will be OK."

He gulped, and my mother stepped forward,

"Jon, your father has something he wants to give to you." Pa looked at my mother doubtfully, and she gave him a gentle push toward the door. He returned a few moments later carrying a bewildered Crest, and delivered him right into my arms.

From the on, not another bird was shot; not for food, nor for profit, nor for pleasure. I was finally able to explain to my father what I really wanted to do with birds; I wanted to take pictures of them in their natural glory. I think my father finally understood, because for my birthday gift, I received a camera, and a card inscribed with the words:

"May all your dreams come true."

By Mary A.G. Embery
Grades 6–8
First Place
Center for Gifted Education Talent Search

Name: ______________________ Date: ______________

THE BLUE HERON

Consequences and Implications

A3

How would the story have been different if the following had happened:

a.) Jon had missed the blue heron?
b.) Jon had not lived after being shot?
c.) Jon had told his father about his desires?
d.) Crest had been shot instead of Jon?

Cause and Effect

A2

Why does Jon get a camera for his birthday at the end of the story?

Sequencing

A1

List the five most important events of the story in order.

Name: ______________________________ Date: ______________

THE BLUE HERON

Generalizations

B3

What generalizations can you make about the following based on the story:

a.) Hunting
b.) People who like to hunt
c.) People who don't like to hunt

Classifications

B2

Classify each set of reasons from B1 into positive and negative using the table below.

Positive Reasons	**Negative Reasons**

Details

B1

What are the reasons for Jon's father wanting to kill the heron?

What are Jon's reasons for not wanting to kill the heron?

Name: ______________________________ Date: ______________

Clay Marbles, Aleksei, and Me

Every night I open my tin box and examine the clay marbles that my little friend Aleksei and I used to play with. As I hold them, I hope the rumors are not true. The Romanoffs must be alive, especially my little friend Aleksei.

I remember the games we used to play with his beautiful glass marbles and my clay marbles. In the afternoon when the kitchen was quiet, I was ordered to take Aleksei a snack and keep him company. Whoever thought Sophia, the kitchen worker, would be allowed to hold the hands of Aleksei Nikolaevich, heir to the Russian throne? Whenever I would visit him I would take milk, cinnamon bread, jam, and marbles. As soon as he finished eating we would play games. These visits were wonderful.

Soon after I started working for the Romanoffs, Aleksei and I became great friends. His parents, Tsar Nicholas and Tsarina Alexandra, encouraged our friendship, so the afternoon visits became a routine. We had to play quietly because Aleksei had hemophilia. I had been told that it is a serious blood disease. Aleksei had four sisters: Olga, Tatiana, Maria, and Anastasia who would sometimes play with us.

I remember one cold afternoon we were shooting marbles into an empty milk cup, when suddenly there was a sharp knock at the door. Aleksei ran to answer it, hoping it was his father. When he opened the door there stood that filthy Grigory Rasputin. Rasputin was a special friend of the Tsar and Tsarina, and supposedly had magical powers. The Imperial Couple felt that these powers controlled hemophilia, so Rasputin was always welcomed.

Aleksei told me that he did not like Rasputin because he was ugly and smelled bad. Rasputin gave orders that he was to examine Aleksei and that I should return to the kitchen. I quickly gathered the dishes on a tray and reluctantly said goodbye to my little friend. As I was walking down the long halls toward the kitchen I kept wondering why Rasputin fascinated the Tsarina. Was it because he could heal her son? I think he was an evil fraud.

I well remember the time Aleksei was watching me bake bread at the winter palace. I received a message that Rasputin would join the family for dinner. Aleksei and I looked at each other and started laughing. We immediately knew I had to make another loaf full of hot spices.

When it was time for dinner each plate was filled with fish, turkey, cabbage, potatoes, spiced apples, and a special slice of bread. While the family was talking and eating, Rasputin suddenly grabbed his throat and started drinking big gulps of cold water. His bread was so spicy that he could hardly talk. He called me to come to the table, grabbed my shoulders and said he had been poisoned. At the far end of the table Aleksei was trying not to giggle.

I told Rasputin that no one in my kitchen would poison him or anyone else. He demanded that I sample his food. After taking small bites of everything, including the bread, he was reassured that he had not been poisoned. I quickly left the room, ran through the kitchen, knocking over a jug of milk, making my way outside to eat handfuls of snow. After that evening Rasputin ate fewer meals at the palace.

Another palace visitor was Eugene Fabergé. Unlike Rasputin, he was an elegant gentleman and always so interesting. He was a royal craftsman and his family had made beautiful and unusual creations for the many Romanoffs. Every Easter the Fabergé family was ordered to design, create, and deliver an Imperial Easter Egg. They were full of jewels and delicate patterns. The special thing about each egg was the surprise inside. The Fabergés had complete control over these egg creations. The Tsar and Tsarina had no idea what the eggs would be like.

The day before an egg delivery the palace was filled with joy. The servants were busy cleaning and cooking special foods. Little Aleksei watched out the window, ready to signal us when he caught sight of the royal automobile coming towards the palace. Preparing for this visitor seemed like a celebration. Eugene Fabergé was kind to everyone in the palace, but he seemed to have a special interest in my dear little Aleksei. Aleksei loved the Imperial Eggs and Fabergé loved telling how they were made.

Name: ______________________ Date: ______________

It was Easter, 1912, when Eugene Fabergé delivered my favorite Imperial Egg. We were staying at the Lividia Palace in Yalta and I remember hearing the Tsar say that Fabergé was traveling across Russia with the newest egg. We all knew he would be exhausted after his journey. His room was in order and we baked his favorite pies.

When he arrived you would have never known that he had come such a very long way. As usual, his attention was focused on Aleksei. He held him in his lap while Tsarina Alexandra opened the new Imperial Easter Egg. Not only was the entire royal family there to see the new masterpiece, but the Tsar allowed the servants to watch as well.

The egg was magnificent. It was blue lapis and gold. The surprise inside was a double-headed eagle with hundreds of diamonds that formed a miniature picture frame around my precious Aleksei. It was a double-sided picture. Not only could you see his beautiful face, but you could see the back of his head. I wanted to have the egg for myself and then I would have Aleksei forever, but all I have are my clay marbles.

My life with the Romanoffs was always an adventure. I traveled to many places, and met unusual people. I was frequently in the company of five beautiful children. All I have to remember them by are my clay marbles and a tin box full of memories of my afternoons with Aleksei.

By Kathleen Brown
Grades 4–5
Honorable Mention
Center for Gifted Education Talent Search

Name: ______________________ Date: ______________

CLAY MARBLES, ALEXSEI, AND ME

B3 Generalizations

What generalizations can you make about the type of person the narrator is?

B2 Classifications

Using the lists you created in B1, create a Venn diagram of the characteristics of the narrator and Rasputin, then Rasputin and Fabergé.

B1 Details

List details about the following characters from the story:

- The narrator
- Rasputin
- Fabergé

Name: ____________________ Date: ____________

CLAY MARBLES, ALEXSEI, AND ME

C3 Theme/Concept

What are some of the concepts explored in the story? What evidence do you have to support your answer?

C2 Inference

If given the opportunity, do you think the narrator would rejoin the family? What evidence supports your position?

C1 Literary Elements

What do you know about Aleksei from this story? What do you know about his family? Support your answer.

Name: ______________________ Date: ______________

The Fox and the Cat

(Originally told by Aesop)

A fox was boasting to a cat about his clever devices for escaping his enemies: "I have a whole bag of tricks," he said, "which contains a hundred ways of escaping my enemies."

"I have only one," said the cat, "but I can generally manage with that." Just at that moment, they heard the cry of a pack of hounds coming towards them, and the cat immediately scampered up a tree and hid herself in the boughs. "This is my plan," said the cat. "What are you going to do?" The fox thought first of one way, then another, and while he was debating the hounds came nearer and nearer. At last, the fox in his confusion was caught up by the hounds and soon killed by the huntsmen.

Name: ______________________ Date: ______________

THE FOX AND THE CAT

B3 Generalizations

Think about the categories you created for the fox's potential means of escape. Now, think about the cat's method of escape. What generalizations can you make about the fox's predicament?

B2 Classifications

Look at the list you created in Question B1. Put the methods of escape that the fox might use into categories.

B1 Details

The fox in the fable boasted about his "whole bag of tricks" for escaping enemies. List at least 25 methods the fox might use to escape.

Name: ______________________ Date: ______________

THE FOX AND THE CAT

Theme/Concept

C3

A sample concept map is started for you about how the story illustrates the concept of "success." Complete the concept map here and then create a concept map of your own on "change," "right and wrong," or another idea.

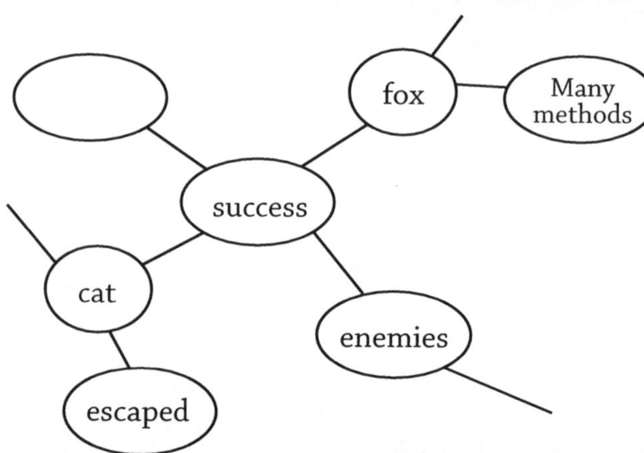

Inference

C2

What inferences can you make about the kind of people the fox and the cat would be if they were human? What evidence from the text supports your inferences?

Literary Elements

C1

Using a Venn diagram, compare and contrast the fox and the cat.

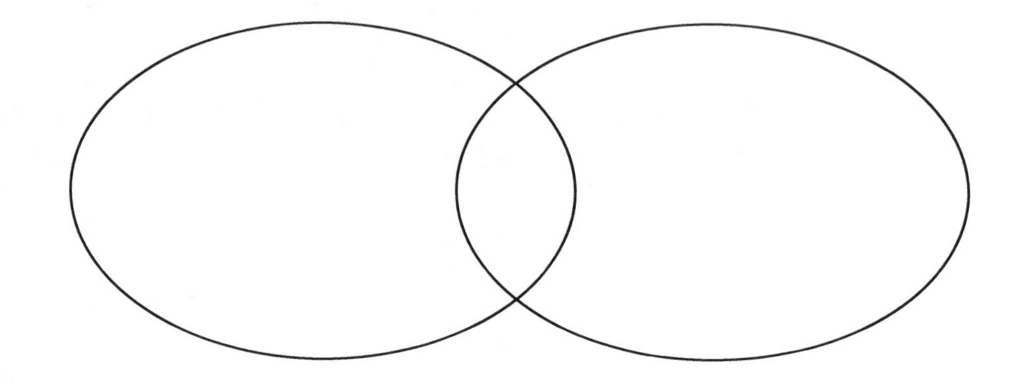

Name: ______________________ Date: ______________

The Lost Wig

(Originally told by Aesop)

A funny old lion, who had the misfortune to lose his mane, was wearing a wig as he was taking a stroll on a very windy day.

Looking up, he spied one of the charming Tiger sisters across the street, and, wishing to make an impression, smiled blandly and made a beautiful low bow. At that moment a very smart gust of wind came up, and the consequence was that his wig flew off and left him there, feeling foolish and looking worse, with his bald head glistening like a billiard ball. Though somewhat embarrassed at first, he smiled at the Lady and said: "Is it a wonder that another fellow's hair shouldn't keep on my head, when my own wouldn't stay there?"

Name: ______________________ Date: ______________

THE LOST WIG

Consequences and Implications

A3

What do you think might happen next in the fable? Defend your ideas.

Cause and Effect

A2

What caused the lion to bow? What was the effect of his actions?

Sequencing

A1

List five events that occur in the fable in order.

Name: ____________________ Date: ____________

C3

Theme/Concept

Write a moral for this fable and defend your choice.

C2

Inference

What do you think the lion expected would happen when he bowed? What evidence supports your answer?

C1

Literary Elements

Draw a picture or write a description of the lion. What are his most important characteristics? Why?

THE LOST WIG

Name: ______________________________ Date: ______________

Mary Poppins' Secret

This document was found in the files of (the author) on September 30, 1997.

April 28, 1956

We all know the story of Mary Poppins. Mary Poppins floats on an umbrella to the house where two children live. She becomes their nanny. She does so-called magic with her so-called magic powers. But nobody knows the truth about her, except Mary Poppins and me.

The truth is, Mary Poppins doesn't have any powers at all! She never has had any, and never will.

Then how did she pull big armchairs out of empty carpetbags? How did she slide up the banister?

It was all my powers, in my fingers. I worked the magic. I didn't get paid, but I *had* to help Mary. You see, I am a magic fairy. Normally, my job is to go around to kids' houses and give them good dreams. But once I used my powers to play a nasty trick: I gave the kids bad dreams instead. So in 1933, I had to begin an apprenticeship with a Fairyland drill instructor—Mary Poppins—to learn how to use my powers properly. Here's how it worked:

Mary's job was to teach discipline to wayward fairies such as myself. The lessons were dull and tiresome. All day long, I had to sit on Mary's shoulder and follow the instructions she had written on a list. Here's an example of a list she gave me on a typical day:

Memo
From: M. Poppins
To: E. Fairy

1. **9:30 a.m.:** Fly me to the general store (I will be using my umbrella to make it look as if the umbrella is doing the actual flying). Fill my shopping basket with cleaning supplies: Crystal Clear glass cleaning spray, paper towels, the smallest toothbrush you can find, and some rags. [Naturally, Mary refused to consider my allergies, which were horribly irritated by that foul smelling Crystal Clear cleaning spray. What was it made out of? Ragweed juice?]
2. **10 a.m.:** After I pay for the items, fly me and all of the items I have with me back to the house. Get out the toothbrush and start working your powers by cleaning all of the windows in the house. [While I was doing this rotten job, dodging spiders and praying mantises and who-knows-what-else, Mary was screaming and yelling at me, ignoring the

fact that the household bugs thought I looked like a perfect morning snack! Later, when Mrs. Banks complimented Mary on the nice job she did on the windows, my "drill instructor" just smiled sweetly and said, "Thank you."]

3. **1 p.m.:** Feed the children. Save the scraps for yourself. Leave nothing for the mice!
4. **1:35 p.m.:** Use your powers to clean up the nursery. Make it look as if I'm doing it. If I snap my fingers at one thing, straighten up or put away that one thing. [Later, Jane and Michael were looking at Mary Poppins in awe when the dollhouse was magically neatened at the snap of Mary's fingers. It was so maddening!]
5. **2:50 p.m.:** Study the Fairy Rule Book until 4:30 sharp. Be prepared for a quiz. Meet me in the nursery.
6. **4:30 p.m.:** Quiz. Failure or cheating will result in an automatic doubling of your apprenticeship. [Believe me, I never studied so hard for anything—not even my very first flying test.]
7. **5 p.m.:** With your powers, fold over the children's bed covers. Again, make it look as if I am doing it. [What did she *think* I was going to do? Make it look as if the dog did it?]
8. **6 p.m.:** In the kitchen, open the oven door and put the turkey in. [When Mrs. Banks turned around and saw the turkey floating to the open oven door, she said, "My, how talented you are, Mary!" I felt like dropping it at Mary's feet.]
9. **7 p.m.:** After the turkey has cooked, put dinner on the table. [Notice she didn't say anything about me eating the scraps or starving the mice or whatever. That's because she always kept turkey leftovers for her hungry old self.]
10. **7:15 p.m.:** Clean the rest of the house. [I was up half the night just picking dirt off the carpet. You would think they had never heard of wiping their feet!]
11. **11:15 p.m.:** You are free until 6:30 sharp tomorrow morning. Meet me in my bedroom to receive the new day's list of chores.

Doesn't sound like much fun, does it? Believe me, it wasn't.

At night, when my work was done, I was too exhausted even to fly. So, I'd drag my little fairy feet down the hall, past the children's nursery, and past Mary Poppins' room. Sometimes I was so miserable I wanted to give her a bad dream. But I knew I would be in big trouble if I did. So, I'd

Name: ______________________ Date: ______________

just go under the table at the end of the hall, where there was a small hole I had made for myself. I would have just enough strength to crawl through the hole and curl up on a mat that was made out of old rags.

Mary Poppins was a strict person. She always expected everything to be done right. If one thing was the tiniest bit of a millimeter wrong, I was banned to 1⁄12 of the food I usually got. I would be starving that day but Mary said it was "good for the character," whatever that meant. So, as you may expect, I worked very hard.

But every once in awhile, I would make a little mistake. Like the time I accidentally used shampoo instead of the children's bubble bath. Mary was furious! She screamed like a maniac and threatened to have my wings tied. Of course, it was an empty threat, because if I didn't have the use of my wings, I would not have been able to help Mary. At the time, though, I was too scared to see through her bullying.

When 1950 came around, Mary came up to me and said in her usual snotty voice, "Erin, you have learned to use your powers correctly. In reward, I will set you free. Another fairy who also used her powers incorrectly now needs a dose of my training. Good-bye."

I ran to get my few meager belongings from my hole in the wall. I flew away fast. When I looked back, there was Mary Poppins, bossing the new fairy around, just as she did me. Then she looked up for a second. I thought I saw just the hint of a tear.

I do not think happily of my days with Mary Poppins; but neither do I regret them. The apprenticeship taught me my lesson. I have never again given any child a bad dream.

Mary, of course, went on to become famous. Some writer started hanging around and watching her while I was there, and later wrote a book about how great Mary supposedly was. I couldn't believe it when people read the book, and actually believed that she was behind all the hocus-pocus stuff. Imagine, an umbrella that can fly! I always wanted to shout out that I was the one with the real talent. I wanted to write my own book. But that is another Fairyland rule. We fairies cannot boast or brag or write books about ourselves. The most we can do is keep diaries, and hope that someone will find them . . .

By Erin Keating
Grades 4–5
First Place
Center for Gifted Education Talent Search

Name: ______________________ Date: ______________

MARY POPPINS' SECRET

C3

Theme/Concept

Why did the narrator share this memo with the world? What ideas does she want to share?

C2

Inference

The narrator claims to have done all of Mary Poppins' work for her. What evidence does the narrator provide to support her claim? What inferences can you make about Mary Poppins based on the story?

C1

Literary Elements

Using a Venn diagram, compare and contrast the characters of Mary Poppins and the narrator of the story.

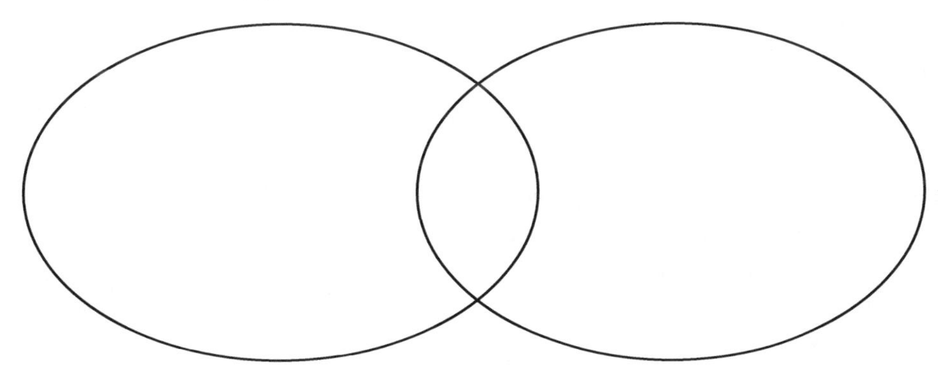

Name: ______________________ Date: ______________

MARY POPPINS' SECRET

Creative Synthesis

D3

The memo in this story is an example of the type of memo E. Fairy would receive from Mary Poppins. Use the memo idea as a model to create your own story about "taking credit for the work of others."

Summarizing

D2

Summarize the main idea of the reading in five sentences or less.

Paraphrasing

D1

Rewrite the following paragraph in your own words:

"Mary, of course, went on to become famous. Some writer started hanging around and watching her while I was there, and later wrote a book about how great Mary supposedly was. I couldn't believe it when people read the book, and actually believed that *she* was behind all the hocus-pocus stuff. Imagine, an umbrella that can fly! I always wanted to shout that I was the one with the real talent. I wanted to write my own book. But that is another Fairyland rule. We fairies cannot boast or brag or write books about ourselves. The most we can do is keep diaries, and hope that someone will find them . . ."

Name: ______________________________ Date: ______________

The Myth of Athena

One day, Metis, wife of Zeus, came to her husband with joyous news: She was going to have a baby. At first, Zeus was ecstatic. He wanted a son or a daughter to whom he could show his power over Greece. However, his enthusiasm for his new son or daughter was short-lived. One of Zeus' trusted advisors told him he should be wary of a child. His advisor asked Zeus, "What if you have a son and your son overthrows you as you overthrew your father?" Zeus became worried. He decided he could not allow Metis to have her child so he swallowed her whole.

After a while, Zeus developed a terrible headache. He was unable to determine the cause of his pain, and his trusted advisor had no answers. The pain continued to increase until one morning Zeus' skull split open! From this chasm, a daughter, Athena emerged. Because Zeus had swallowed Metis whole, he also had absorbed all of her wisdom. The combined wisdom of Zeus and Metis was passed on to Athena who became the goddess of wisdom.

Athena led a very exciting life. In addition to being the goddess of wisdom, Athena also became known as the goddess of war. She helped many of the heroes of the Trojan War achieve victory through her tactical knowledge and the strategies of war.

Athena was revered by the Greeks for her wisdom and is credited with many important inventions such as the wagon, the flute, shoemaking, shipbuilding, and the plough. Through the years, Greeks and their successors have said Athena provided mankind with all of the necessary knowledge to build the foundation of a civilization.

Name: ______________________ Date: ____________

THE MYTH OF ATHENA

Consequences and Implications

A3

Choose three of the inventions that are credited to Athena. How would life be different if these inventions did not exist? Explain your answer.

Cause and Effect

A2

Why did Athena have so much wisdom? Support your answer with evidence from the text.

Sequencing

A1

List the five most important events of the myth in order.

Name: ______________________ Date: ______________

THE MYTH OF ATHENA

Creative Synthesis

D3

Create your own story that explains how wisdom can win wars.

Summarizing

D2

Summarize how being the goddess of wisdom would be helpful to Athena in her role as goddess of war.

Paraphrasing

D1

In your own words, explain why Athena was revered by the Greeks.

Name: ______________________________ Date: ________________

The Myth of Heracles (Hercules)

Heracles (known as Hercules to the Romans) was the son of the god Zeus. When he was a baby, the goddess Hera was jealous of the attention he was given; she sent two serpents to his crib to kill him. Shortly after the serpents were sent, Heracles was found babbling happily with a strangled serpent in each hand. This event was the first clue of Heracles' superhuman strength.

As he grew older, Heracles became a champion marksman and wrestler. Unfortunately, he was driven mad by Hera and in a frenzy of anger killed his own children. To atone for this terrible deed, Heracles was charged with completing 12 tasks, or labors, for his cousin, King Eurystheus. The 12 labors were thought to be impossible; everyone believed Heracles would die trying to accomplish them.

The first labor Heracles was given was to slay the lion Nemean. This lion was no ordinary lion. Arrows or spears could not penetrate his skin. Heracles defeated the lion by blocking the entrance to his den and killing him with his bare hands. When Heracles returned carrying the defeated Nemean, everyone, including Eurystheus, was in awe of his strength.

One of the more exciting tasks for Heracles was to slay the much-feared Hydra. No one is entirely sure how many heads the Hydra had; some believe it was 8 or 9, while others claim the Hydra had 10,000 heads! There was agreement, though, about the Hydra's ability to regrow two heads for every one that was cut off. As if many heads were not frightening enough, the Hydra's breath was lethal to mere mortals. Fortunately for Heracles, he was not a mere mortal. With the help of his nephew, Ialous (who just happened to be waiting in the chariot), Heracles cut off each of the Hydra's

Name: ______________________________ Date: ______________

heads while Ialous seared the wound, making it impossible for another head to grow.

Heracles' final task was to bring back Cerberus from the Underworld, the land of the dead. His first obstacle was getting across the River Styx, the most famous river of the Underworld where all of the dead souls congregated. Heracles could not pay the bribe to Charon the Boatman, nor was he dead; both of these were prerequisites for entering the Underworld. Heracles had to use his superhuman strength to frighten Charon into taking him across the River Styx. Once in the Underworld, Heracles was confronted with Cerberus and his razor-sharp teeth and venomous snake tail. Luckily, Heracles was wearing the armor he made from the lion Nemean that he had slain during the first labor. The lion's skin was impenetrable to the Cerberus' teeth or tail. Heracles eventually succeeded at this labor as well.

Many years later after many more adventures, Heracles died from wearing a tunic tainted by poison, much to the dismay of his beloved wife Deianara.

Name: ______________________________ Date: ______________

THE MYTH OF HERACLES (HERCULES)

Consequences and Implications

A3

Why was Heracles' manner of death ironic? Explain.

Cause and Effect

A2

What caused Heracles to be tasked with the 12 labors? What effects did the assignment have on his life?

Sequencing

A1

List the five most important events in the myth in order.

Name: ______________________________ Date: ______________

THE MYTH OF HERACLES (HERCULES)

D3 — Creative Synthesis

Create a myth that has a crime and punishment theme like the Heracles myth.

D2 — Summarizing

In three sentences or less, summarize the main idea of the myth.

D1 — Paraphrasing

In your own words, rewrite one of the labors described in the myth.

Name: ______________________ Date: ______________

Theseus and the Minotaur

Theseus and his father, King Aegeus, were very close. One day, while they were enjoying the pleasant scenery in the palace garden, a woman came to visit King Aegeus. She begged the king not to send her son to Crete. Not understanding why the woman was asking his father for her son's salvation, Theseus asked the king why the boy would have to go to Crete. King Aegeus explained to his son that every year King Minos, ruler of Crete, demanded seven boys and seven girls be sent to him from Athens for the Minotaur. Theseus asked what King Minos did with the young people sent to him. King Aegeus responded that, unfortunately, he did not know. All of the boys and girls who had been sent to Crete had never been heard from again.

Theseus took a few moments to think about what his father had said. Then, he placed his hands on the woman's shoulders and told her not to worry. Her son would not be going to Crete because he, Theseus, would go in his place. King Aegeus became distraught. "You cannot go!" he exclaimed to Theseus. "You must become king one day." Theseus told his father that he would grow up to be a much better king if he were able to save Athens from King Minos' demands. "I will go to Crete and slay the Minotaur!" cried Theseus.

The next morning, Theseus was preparing for his voyage. His father came to him to explain why his ship had a black sail. If Theseus was successful in slaying the Minotaur, he was to change the sail to white. Everyday, King Aegeus would stand on the cliff overlooking the sea, watching for his son's ship to return. If the sail was white, he would know Theseus had been successful; if the sail was black, he would know Theseus had been slaughtered.

For many days the ship sailed until it finally arrived at Crete. All the people of Crete had gathered to see Theseus' arrival. In the crowd was King Minos' daughter, Ariadne. When she saw Theseus, she immediately fell in love with him. She knew of her father's plans to feed Theseus to the Minotaur; she also knew she could not let Theseus be killed.

Late that night, Ariadne came to Theseus' cell. She told him to follow her very quietly. Ariadne took Theseus to the labyrinth where the Minotaur lived. "Always turn to the right—that is the secret of the labyrinth," said Ariadne. Then, she handed him a sword and a spool of golden thread to mark his path as he went further and further into the maze. Theseus remembered Ariadne's words and always turned to the right. He could hear the Minotaur's roaring growing louder and louder. Suddenly, the

Name: ______________________________ Date: ________________

Minotaur was before him! Theseus attacked, plunging the sword deep into the heart of the ferocious beast. Once he was sure the Minotaur no longer lived, Theseus followed the golden thread out of the labyrinth and into the waiting arms of his beloved Ariadne.

Theseus and Ariadne knew King Minos would be furious when he discovered what had happened. They rapidly ran to Theseus' ship and began the journey back to Athens. King Minos' men quickly began their pursuit and for many hours Theseus was uncertain of their escape from the ships of Crete. Finally, they appeared to have outrun King Minos' men. Ariadne, Theseus, and the crew of the ship decided to spend the night on the island of Naxos. In the morning, however, one of the shipmen saw the ships from Crete approaching. They were once again in danger of being captured. Everyone rushed to the ship and quickly set sail. After outrunning King Minos' men again, Theseus realized that Ariadne had been left on the island of Naxos. He desperately wanted to go back for her, but his men convinced him they would all be captured and killed if they turned back. Saddened, Theseus told his shipmates to continue sailing toward Athens.

In all the excitement, Theseus had forgotten to change the sail from black to white. King Aegeus, who had kept his word and watched for his son everyday from the cliff overlooking the sea, saw the black sail and began to despair. Deciding he did not want to continue living if his son had been killed by the Minotaur, King Aegeus flung himself off the cliff and into the sea (which, to this day, is known as the Aegean sea).

Name: ____________________ Date: ____________

THESEUS AND THE MINOTAUR

Generalizations

B3

What generalizations about bravery can you write using the list and categories you created? How do the generalizations you created apply to this story?

Classifications

B2

Using the list you generated in question B1, create categories of the different ways someone can be brave. Use all of the items from your list.

Details

B1

Theseus acted bravely in this myth by facing the Minotaur. List at least 25 different ways a person can be brave.

Name: ______________________ Date: ______________

THESEUS AND THE MINOTAUR

Creative Synthesis

D3

In ancient times, the same myth was often told from multiple points of view. Retell the myth of "Theseus and the Minotaur" from another character's point of view (e.g., Ariadne, King Minos, King Aegeus).

Summarizing

D2

In five sentences or less, summarize the main ideas of this myth.

Paraphrasing

D1

In your own words, retell what happened to Theseus while he was on the island of Crete.

Chapter 2

Poetry

Chapter 2 includes the selected readings and accompanying question sets for each poetry selection. Each reading is followed by two sets of questions; each set is aligned to one of the four ladder skills. For *Jacob's Ladder 2,* the skills covered by each selection are as follows:

Poetry:	Ladder Skills
A Bedtime Story	C, C
Cousin for Sale	B, C
Grapefruit	B, C
Lift Every Voice and Sing	B, D
My Shadow	B, C
My Sister is a Sissy	B, C
Occupant of Room #709	B, C
Overpopulation	A, C
School House is A Rockin'	B, C
Untitled	B, C

Name: ______________________ Date: ______________

A Bedtime Story

"Tell me a story,"
Says Witch's Child.
About the Beast
So fierce and wild
About a Ghost
That shrieks and groans.
A Skeleton
That rattles bones
About a Monster
Crawly-creepy
Something nice
To make me sleepy!

By Melanie F. Paret
Grades 4–5
Second Place
Center for Gifted Education Talent Search

Name: ______________________ Date: ______________

A BEDTIME STORY

Theme/Concept

C3

Pretend you are collecting poems that are similar to this one to put in a book of poetry. Create a title for the book of poems and create titles for at least four more poems that would belong in a group with this poem. Explain why you chose the titles.

Inference

C2

Infer means "to draw a conclusion based on evidence." From the poem, what can you infer about the witch's child? What is the evidence to support your inferences?

Literary Elements

C1

Point of view refers to the stance of the storyteller. From whose point of view is this poem written? How do you know?

Name: ______________________ Date: ______________

A BEDTIME STORY

Theme/Concept

C3

Using the poem as a model, write your own poem called "Bedtime Story" that begins: "Tell me a story," Says the _____'s Child. Fill in the blank with the name of an animal, person, or other being. Then continue to create a 12-line poem.

Inference

C2

What can you infer about the witch's child? Why does he or she want to be told a story?

Literary Elements

C1

Imagery is the use of words or phrases that appeal to any sense or any combination of senses. You can close your eyes and see the image behind the words of the poet. What images do you see from the poem?

Name: ______________________ Date: ______________

Cousin for Sale

Cousin for sale, cousin for sale,
A whiny, bratty cousin for sale.
She wets the bed,
And she always copies whatever I said.
She'll follow you and bother you,
And she'll want to do whatever you do.
She'll wake you up in the middle of the night,
And start a stupid pillow fight.

Cousin for sale, cousin for sale,
A stupid, clumsy cousin for sale.
She spills her milk, eats like a hog,
She always scared my little pet dog.
She falls off her bike, and cries and cries,
Until you just want to die.
You will regret it if you don't let her follow you around,
At least if you get her ice cream she won't make a sound.
If you are tired, she'll want to play store,
If you say you don't want to, she'll just cry for more.

Cousin for sale, cousin for sale,
A selfish, childish cousin for sale.
When she wants to do something, you can't say no,
If you try to leave, she won't let you go.
She'll want to put your hair in little pink bows.
She'll only wear ugly pink clothes.
She won't eat the vegetables that you cook,
She won't go to bed without you reading her a book.

Cousin for sale, cousin for sale,
A messy, disgusting cousin for sale.
She wets her pants, oh no, what a mess,
She just got hot chocolate on her dress.
She'll pick up worms, then give you a hug,
She wants a cookie, she just picked up a bug.
She drools when she is asleep,
What a mess on her new stuffed sheep.
You can't get through breakfast without something on the floor,
She makes a messy handprint on the window by the door.

Name: ______________________________ Date: ______________

Cousin for sale, cousin for sale,
A loud, obnoxious cousin for sale.
When Barney comes on she screams with delight,
If she doesn't get her way, she will pick a fight.
When she saw *E.T.* she screamed and cried,
She really thought E.T. was going to die.
So, if you don't want to hear a little girl holler,
Then buying this kid, I wouldn't bother!

By Brooke A. Shormaker
Grades 4–5
Honorable Mention
Center for Gifted Education Talent Search

Name: ______________________________ Date: ______________

COUSIN FOR SALE

B3

Generalizations

Using the titles you created from for your groups in B2, write at least three generalizations you can make about the cousin as a person. Use evidence from the poem.

B2

Classifications

Look over your list of characteristics. Divide them into groups and create a title for each group of characteristics.

B1

Details

Make a list of characteristics of this cousin who is for sale.

Name: ______________________ Date: ______________

Cousin for Sale

C3 Theme/Concept

Think about the events described in the poem from the point of view of the young cousin. Using "Cousin for Sale" as a model, write a new poem from the young cousin's point of view. For example, in the last stanza: "When she saw *E.T.* she screamed and cried," could become: "When I saw *E.T.*, I was so scared!" The poem should be at least 16 lines long.

C2 Inference

What feelings do you think the author has about her cousin? Why? Use phrases from the poem as evidence to support your inference.

C1 Literary Elements

Think of a young child you know who is about the same age as the cousin in the poem. Using the characterization of the cousin who is for sale, create a Venn diagram and compare and contrast the author's cousin to the young child you know. Label the left circle with the name of the child you know. Label the right circle with "The cousin." In the parts of the circles that do not overlap, write characteristics that tell how the two children are different. In the middle, where the two circles overlap, write characteristics of the two children that are the same.

Name: ______________________________ Date: ______________

Grapefruit

Mellow orb,
Sunny and cheerful,
Full of light,
Broad and square.

Sliced in half like a magician's stunt.
Tart, yet slightly sweet,
Concealed inside a mellow mask.

A sister to a coconut,
Soaking up the sun,
Keeping its secret sealed inside to share with everyone.

By Emily P. Rapoport
Grades 6–8
Honorable Mention
Center for Gifted Education Talent Search

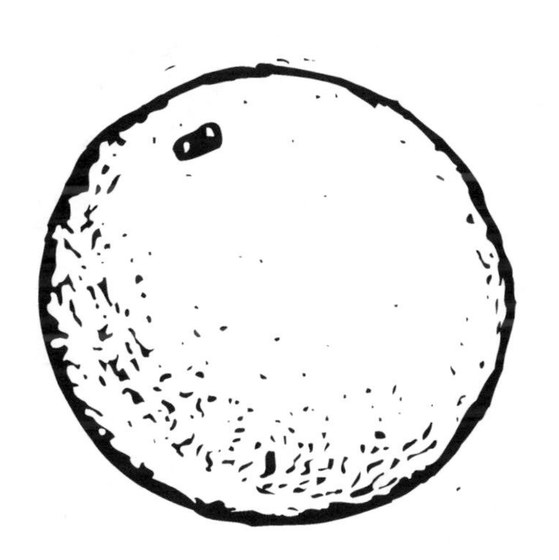

Name: ________________________ Date: ____________

GRAPEFRUIT

Generalizations

B3

What can you generalize about the use of describing words in a poem or story? How would stories or poems change if authors used too many or too few describing words?

Classifications

B2

Sort the describing words and phrases from B1 into categories. Give each category a title.

Details

B1

List the characteristics of a grapefruit using the words and phrases in the poem. Look up any words that are unfamiliar to you.

Name: ______________________ Date: ______________

GRAPEFRUIT

C3

Theme/Concept

You are going to write a poem. Select an object in your classroom. That will be the title of the poem. Brainstorm words and phrases you can use to describe that object, including "people" attributes (personification). Write your poem using the words and phrases you brainstormed to explain your object. Read your poem to the class, without saying the title of your poem, and ask them to guess your title.

C2

Inference

Write each line of the poem. Next to the line, explain how that line is a clue to describing the title object.

C1

Literary Elements

Personification is a figure of speech that gives human characteristics to nonhuman objects. Give examples of personification from the poem.

Name: ______________________ Date: ______________

Lift Every Voice and Sing

By James W. Johnson

Lift every voice and sing
Till earth and heaven ring,
Ring with the harmonies of Liberty;
Let our rejoicing rise
High as the listening skies,
Let it resound loud as the rolling sea.
Sing a song full of the faith that the dark past has taught us,
Sing a song full of the hope that the present has brought us,
Facing the rising sun of our new day begun
Let us march on till victory is won.
Stony the road we trod,
Bitter the chastening rod,
Felt in the days when hope unborn had died;
Yet with a steady beat,
Have not our weary feet
Come to the place for which our fathers sighed?
We have come over a way that with tears has been watered,
We have come, treading our path through the blood of the slaughtered,
Out from the gloomy past,
Till now we stand at last
Where the white gleam of our bright star is cast.
God of our weary years,
God of our silent tears,
Thou who has brought us thus far on the way;
Thou who has by Thy might
Led us into the light,
Keep us forever in the path, we pray.
Lest our feet stray from the places, our God, where we met Thee,
Lest, our hearts drunk with the wine of the world, we forget Thee;
Shadowed beneath Thy hand,
May we forever stand.
True to our God,
True to our native land.

Name: ______________________ Date: ______________

LIFT EVERY VOICE AND SING

B3

Generalizations

Write one generalization about the author's view of the past. Write one generalization about the author's view of the present.

B2

Classifications

Make a T-chart. Label one side "sorrow" and the other side "joy." Find phrases from the poem that communicate these two feelings. Sort them into the two categories and put them on the chart.

Sorrow	**Joy**

B1

Details

This poem refers to two time periods: now and sometime in the past. Make a list of words that help the reader know the author is writing about now. Make another list of words that help the reader know the author is writing about the past.

Now	**Then**

Name: ____________________ Date: ____________

LIFT EVERY VOICE AND SING

D3 Creative Synthesis

Use the first stanza of the poem as a model for writing a new poem. For the first line of the new poem, use the opening line of the original poem: "Lift every voice and sing," then use "Let us march on till victory is won" as the last line of your new poem.

D2 Summarizing

In just a few sentences, summarize the main ideas of the poem.

D1 Paraphrasing

Reread the second stanza. Use your own words to explain each line. Remember, sometimes a sentence is inverted: "A dog have I" means "I have a dog." This poet uses inverted sentences many times. Use a dictionary to look up any words that are unfamiliar.

Name: ______________________ Date: ______________

My Shadow

By Robert Louis Stevenson

I have a little shadow that goes in and out with me,
And what can be the use of him is more than I can see.
He is very, very like me from the heels up to the head;
And I see him jump before me, when I jump into my bed.

The funniest thing about him is the way he likes to grow—
Not at all like proper children, which is always very slow;
For he sometimes shoots up taller like an India-rubber ball,
And he sometimes goes so little that there's none of him at all.

He hasn't got a notion of how children ought to play,
And can only make a fool of me in every sort of way.
He stays so close behind me, he's a coward you can see;
I'd think shame to stick to nursie as that shadow sticks to me!

One morning, very early, before the sun was up,
I rose and found the shining dew on every buttercup;
But my lazy little shadow, like an arrant sleepy-head,
Had stayed at home behind me and was fast asleep in bed.

Name: ______________________ Date: ______________

MY SHADOW

Generalizations

B3

Write one or two generalizations about shadows.

Classifications

B2

Create categories using the words and phrases from Activity B1. Every word and phrase must fit into one and only one category. Create a title for each group.

Details

B1

Make a list of words and phrases that are used to describe the shadow.

Name: ______________________ Date: ______________

MY SHADOW

Theme/Concept

C3

Write one or two sentences that explain what ideas the author wanted to share with his readers.

Inference

C2

Make a list of characteristics of a shadow noted in the poem. What inferences can you make about the "character" of the shadow from these characteristics?

Literary Elements

C1

Personification is the process of creating an object or animal that has human characteristics. Robert Louis Stevenson uses personification in this poem. How does the child describe his shadow to reflect personification?

Name: ______________________________ Date: ________________

My Sister Is a Sissy

My sister is a sissy, she's afraid of dogs and cats.
She positively shivers at the shadows of some bats.
She is afraid of things with fur and fluffy feathers too.
If you are big and ugly, she is even scared of you.
But I won't tease my sister for her fears of scales and fur.
For while she is scared of all of them, I am scared of her.

By Andy P. Fram
Grades 4–5
Honorable Mention
Center for Gifted Education Talent Search

Name: ______________________ Date: ____________

MY SISTER IS A SISSY

B3 Generalizations

What can you generalize about fears from the poem? (Use your answers from B1 and B2 to help you.)

B2 Classifications

The things the sister is afraid of can be classified as animals or people. Look at your list and create categories of things you fear. Label each category with a word that describes that list.

B1 Details

Give examples of things the sister is afraid of. Make a list of things that scare you. How are the lists alike? Different?

Name: ______________________ Date: ______________

MY SISTER IS A SISSY

Theme/Concept

C3

Create an alternative title that might be seen as focusing on a major idea in the poem.

Inference

C2

Is the sister a sissy? Why or why not? Use evidence from the poem to explain your answer.

Literary Elements

C1

Alliteration is the repetition of the beginning consonant sound in words. Make a list of examples of alliteration from this poem.

Name: ______________________________ Date: ______________

Occupant of Room #709

She is old
and her dancing feet just don't move
like they used to
she can hear the ragtime jig
and the faint beat
but her hips just can't do the woo-woo

Now-a-days
she stares off and remembers
those summer dances
with all the young club members
on sticky humid nights
when she'd flip her auburn hair
and feel her light silk skirt
be teased by the night's cool air.

She was young then
and her dancing feet
would dance until they were black and blue
to the ragtime jigs and the swinging beats
when her hips could do the woo-woo.

By Nicole L. Hannans
Grades 9–12
First Place: Poetry
Center for Gifted Education Talent Search

Name: ______________________ Date: ______________

OCCUPANT OF ROOM #709

B3

Generalizations

Using your list as a guide, make two general statements about the woman.

B2

Classifications

Using your list of details, are there any inferences you can make to classify this woman?

B1

Details

What details do we know about the character from the poem?

Name: ______________________________ Date: ______________

OCCUPANT OF ROOM #709

C3

Theme/Concept

What important idea about life does this poem tell us?

C2

Inference

Poems often create feelings in the reader. What feelings does this poem create? Give examples of words from the poem that create these feelings. What inferences can you make about how the use of certain words in a poem help create mood?

C1

Literary Elements

The author compares and contrasts the past and the present in this poem. Write a paragraph describing the character from the poem as she was in the past and as she is in the present.

Name: ______________________ Date: ______________

Overpopulation

Another kid is born every couple of seconds
Bringing the worldwide population up
Cramming the world with more and more people
Destroying animal houses to make our own
Endangered animals become extinct
For people need more and more space
Going and destroying nature
Habitat destruction harms tons of animals
In the world, animals are going extinct
Jaguars and pandas are endangered
Koalas and rhinos are right alongside them
Loads of people lead to global warming
More heat in the air is dispersed every second
North and South Poles are melting
On the Earth we should all live in harmony
Place your car aside and ride a bike
Quickly decide to save the Earth
Reduce the carbon dioxide
Slow down the speed of the polar ice caps melting
Try and not use electricity too often
Understand the damage we have done
We all need to help save the world
X-treme amount of damage we need to restore
Years should go by with no more harm
Zest about saving the world should be spread around

By Colin van 't Veld
Originally published in Creative Kids *magazine*
Summer 2008
Reprinted with permission by Prufrock Press Inc.

Name: ______________________ Date: ______________

A3

Consequences and Implications

In the first part of the poem the author describes the consequences of overpopulation and in the second part of the poem the author describes a plan of action. Think of an issue you are concerned about. Write your own ABC poem, using "Overpopulation" as a model. Make sure your poem flows.

A2

Cause and Effect

Create a fishbone diagram to show the effects of overpopulation. Use evidence from the poem as your guide. A sample diagram has been started for you.

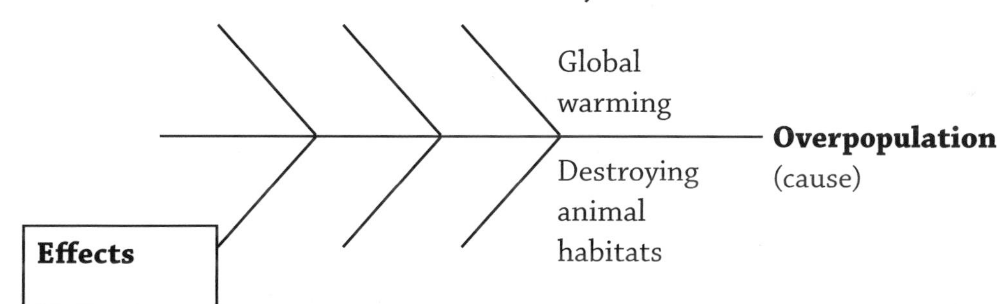

A1

Sequencing

What possible solutions does the author suggest to help with overpopulation?

OVERPOPULATION

Name: ______________________ Date: ______________

OVERPOPULATION

Theme/Concept

C3

Using the evidence the author provides and other information you know about overpopulation, write a friendly letter to a Senator or other public official discussing the issue of overpopulation from the point of view of an animal or plant.

Inference

C2

What does the author mean by "Zest about saving the world should be spread around" (last line)?

Literary Elements

C1

How does the author characterize the Earth right now? How do you know?

Name: ______________________________ Date: ______________

School House Is A Rockin'

School house is a rockin'
While the principal is a knockin'.
The teachers are a dancin'
And the chairs are a prancin'.
While the principal is a knockin'
And the school house is a rockin'.
The children are a jigglin'
And the desks are a wigglin'
While the chairs are a prancin';
And the teachers are a dancin'
And the principal is a knockin'
And the school house is a rockin'.
The phone in the main office is a ringin'
off the hook
And the parents are a worried
And all the other people want to take a look at . . .
The school house that's a rockin'
And the principal that's a knockin'
And the teachers that are a dancin'
And the chairs that are a prancin'
While the children are a jigglin'
And the desks are a wigglin'
Oh by the way, I am the secretary in the
main office that's a pourin' tea.
And I am as mad as a bear with no honey
'Cause they won't take a look at me.

By Amanda C. Huskin
Grades 4–5
Third Place
Center for Gifted Education Talent Search

Name: ____________________ Date: ____________

SCHOOL HOUSE IS A ROCKIN'

Generalizations

B3

Focus on the actions of each group. Write three generalizations about the actions in the poem.

Classifications

B2

Group these actions into categories and give each group a title that describes the actions.

Details

B1

Make a list of the characters from the poem and what each character is doing.

Name: ____________________ Date: ____________

C3

Theme/Concept

After reading this poem, what ideas do you think the author has about school?

C2

Inference

Looking at the repetition and the way each line of the poem ends, describe the feeling you think the author wants the reader to have. What words from the poem support your ideas?

C1

Literary Elements

Repetition is a device used in poetry to repeat words, lines, phrases, or stanzas. Make a list of examples of repetition from the poem.

SCHOOL HOUSE IS A ROCKIN'

Name: ______________________________ Date: ______________

Untitled

Dancing in the wind
there was a little seed
who had nothing to give,
or to want or to need.
But she knew she would never be a weed
So she just danced in the wind in rain or shine,
and landed in my garden and became a flower of mine.

By Alyssa M. Argenzio
Grades 4–5
Honorable Mention
Center for Gifted Education Talent Search

Name: ______________________ Date: ______________

B3

Generalizations

Which generalization best describes the poem?

a) Seeds dance and play.
b) Everyone has something to give.
c) April showers bring May flowers.

Why did you select your answer? Use words from the poem to explain your choice in a well-developed paragraph.

B2

Classifications

Create a T-chart. On the left, list phrases the author used to personify the seed. On the right, list characteristics of seeds that may have caused the author to choose each phrase on the left. Now do the same thing with your list from B1.

Phrases describing seeds	Characteristics of seeds

Details

Choose an object, like the seed in the poem, and make a list of human characteristics you would give to your object if you were writing a poem about it.

Name: ______________________ Date: ______________

UNTITLED

C3

Theme/Concept

This author chose not to create a title for this poem. Create a title that reveals the main idea of the poem.

C2

Inference

Using the words the author chose, what can we infer about the seed's attitude about life?

C1

Literary Elements

Personification is a figure of speech that gives animals or objects human characteristics. Make a list of human characteristics the author gave this little seed.

Chapter 3

Nonfiction

Chapter 3 includes the selected readings and accompanying question sets for each nonfiction selection. Each reading is followed by two sets of questions; each set is aligned to one of the four ladder skills. For *Jacob's Ladder 2,* the skills covered by each selection are as follows:

Nonfiction:	**Ladder Skills**
The American Revolutionary War	C, D
The Exploration of Space	A, D
Graphic Ice Cream	B, C
The Great Depression	A, B
It's Electric	B, D
The Metric System vs. the U.S. Customary System	A, C

Name: ______________________ Date: ____________

The American Revolutionary War

In 1765, Americans still considered themselves loyal subjects to the British crown. Great Britain had just finished the Seven Years War with France, during which the Americans helped the British defeat the French on American soil. After the war ended, Great Britain was looking for a way to help pay for the war. Because part of the reason they went to war with France was to protect their colonies in America, the British government decided to pay for the war through taxing Americans. The taxes implemented by the British government were not necessarily high. However, Americans were upset that they were not consulted about the new taxes. The Americans felt it was illegal, or at the very least not fair, to tax them without giving them proper representation within the British parliament. The statement "No taxation without representation" became a well-known phrase during the American Revolutionary War.

The first direct tax against the colonies was the Stamp Act in 1765. The Stamp Act declared that all official documents, newspapers, almanacs, pamphlets, and even playing cards must have official stamps on them. If they did not have stamps, which Americans must buy from Britain, then fines would be charged. Later acts further restricted the activities of Americans. The Currency Act prohibited Americans from printing their own paper money, which hindered trade among the colonies. The Quartering Act mandated that American colonists house British soldiers in their homes, which invaded the colonists' privacy. Colonists began voicing their protests against these taxes and acts. In 1770, the Boston Massacre occurred in Massachusetts. In protest of the Stamp Act and the Tea Act, colonists dumped tea bricks from British ships into Boston Harbor, in what is now known as the Boston Tea Party. During this protest, five Americans were killed.

Because of incidents like this one, as well as philosophical differences between England and the colonies, and America's desire for independence, the American Revolutionary War, also known as the American War of Independence, began in 1775.

In 1776, representatives from each of the 13 colonies met in Philadelphia where they unanimously signed the Declaration of Independence, thereby forming the United States of America. In 1778, the colonists formed an alliance with France. The French helped by sending money, munitions, and troops. These contributions from France helped level the playing field in the war against Britain. However, the Americans were fighting against a monarchy for the right to establish a democracy. Even though France was helping them win their independence, Americans did not view France as a role model.

During the war, only ⅓ of the colonists, known as Patriots, supported war with Britain, ⅓ of colonists, known as Loyalists, remained loyal to Britain, and ⅓ of colonists remained neutral. However, throughout the war, the Patriots maintained control over 80–90% of the land. The British were able to capture only a few coastal cities, which they gained through their strong Navy presence.

At the Battle at Saratoga in 1777, one of Britain's main armies was captured, the beginning of the end for the British. In 1781, the British army surrendered at the Battle of Yorktown. This surrender led to the signing of the Treaty of Paris for peace in 1783.

Name: ______________________________ Date: ______________

THE AMERICAN REVOLUTIONARY WAR

Theme/Concept

C3

For what concept was the American Revolutionary War fought? State your answer in five words or less.

Inference

C2

What inferences can be made about the French becoming allies with the Americans during the American Revolutionary War? Justify your answer.

Literary Elements

C1

Choose to be a Patriot, a Loyalist, or a neutral colonist. Describe your character's point of view regarding the war. Support your answer with details.

Name: ______________________ Date: ______________

THE AMERICAN REVOLUTIONARY WAR

D3

Creative Synthesis

Write a letter to your family about the American Revolutionary War from the point of view of a colonist, a British soldier, or a French soldier. Be sure to include enough details for the recipient of your letter to understand the war from your point of view.

D2

Summarizing

In three sentences or less, summarize the cause(s) of the American Revolutionary War.

D1

Paraphrasing

In your own words, rewrite the following statements:

(a) "No taxation without representation."

(b) "Even though France was helping them win their independence, Americans did not view France as a role model."

Name: ____________________ Date: ____________

The Exploration of Space

The exploration of space gives scientists the opportunity to learn about the sun, stars, and planets. Some space exploration involves scientists called *astronauts* traveling into space. Astronauts use spacecraft, such as space shuttles, to travel beyond the Earth's atmosphere into outer space, which begins about 60 miles above the surface of the Earth. While in outer space, astronauts explore their surroundings with various tools such as jet-powered backpacks called *manned maneuvering units*, or MMUs. MMUs allow astronauts to move around outside their spacecraft without a safety line attached. Other space exploration does not require astronauts but instead uses spacecraft with robots or other mechanical devices, such as satellites, to gather information.

In order for spacecraft, manned or unmanned, to travel into outer space, they must first overcome the pull of Earth's gravity. The heavier an object, the more power is required to break the Earth's gravitational pull. As you can imagine, it takes a tremendous amount of power to launch a space shuttle. These large spacecraft require booster rockets full of fuel to launch them. The boosters burn the fuel that gives off gas bursts that push the spacecraft into the air. The spacecraft eventually reaches a height where the Earth's gravitational pull no longer affects it. Once it passes this point, the shuttle only needs to fire rockets to increase its speed or to change directions.

When a spacecraft is ready to return to Earth, it must first slow down. Once it re-enters the atmosphere, it slows down considerably and begins falling toward Earth. The spacecraft deploys, or puts into action, parachutes that further slow down its descent. Spacecraft like space shuttles land on runways just like airplanes. Some of the earlier U.S. spacecraft "splashed down" in the ocean where the astronauts were picked up by boats.

Space exploration began on October 4, 1957, when the Soviet Union launched the satellite Sputnik to orbit the Earth. Four years later, on April 12, 1961, the Soviet cosmonaut Yuri A. Gagarin was the first person to travel into space. The first visit to the moon happened in December 1968 when the U.S. spacecraft Apollo 8 orbited the moon 10 times before returning to Earth. Then, on July 20, 1969, the American astronaut Neil Armstrong became the first person to walk on the moon. While placing the American flag on the moon, Armstrong said, "This is one small step for a man, one giant leap for mankind."

Since this historic landing on the moon, astronauts have continued to explore space by traveling there and by studying the data collected by satellites and other unmanned spacecraft. Through space exploration, astronauts and scientists have learned and continue to learn much about the universe beyond Earth.

Name: ______________________ Date: ______________

THE EXPLORATION OF SPACE

Consequences and Implications

A3

What are the implications of space exploration? Support your answer.

Cause and Effect

A2

What is the effect of the Earth's gravitational pull on spacecraft during launch? During reentry? Support your answer with evidence from the text.

Sequencing

A1

Create a timeline of the history of space exploration as presented in the text.

Name: ______________________________ Date: ______________

THE EXPLORATION OF SPACE

Creative Synthesis

D3

Imagine you are an astronaut on the Apollo 8 spacecraft. Write a letter home describing the experience. Be sure to include plenty of details so the recipient of your letter feels like he or she was there with you.

Summarizing

D2

In three sentences or less, describe the different ways scientists and astronauts explore space.

Paraphrasing

D1

In your own words, explain what Neil Armstrong meant when he said, "This is one small step for a man, one giant leap for mankind."

Name: ______________________________ Date: ______________

Graphic Ice Cream

Tim and Lauren, the owners of Crema, an ice cream shop in Raleigh, NC, surveyed their customers about their favorite ice cream flavors, gathered information about the number of customers on each day of the week, and asked their employees to keep track of how they spend their work hours. They then used different kinds of graphs to represent these data.

Over the period of one month, the Crema owners asked their customers to choose their favorite flavors from a list including chocolate, vanilla, strawberry, banana toffee, strawberry cheesecake, blueberry almond, chocolate raspberry, coffee almond, peach pecan, and caramel pecan. The results are presented in Table 1.

Table 1
Customers' Favorite Flavors

Ice Cream Flavor	Number of Customers' Favorite Flavor
Chocolate	120
Vanilla	65
Strawberry	85
Banana Toffee	190
Strawberry Cheesecake	275
Blueberry Almond	135
Chocolate Raspberry	200
Coffee Almond	95
Peach Pecan	150
Caramel Pecan	75

Tim and Lauren then decided to graph the data they had gathered from their customers. They chose to graph the favorite flavors on a bar graph. A bar graph shows the relationships between groups. On a bar graph, one bar is not affected by another. Bar graphs are a good way to show large differences in results from surveys. They also are excellent tools for determining trends. By using a bar graph to represent the data about customers' favorite flavors, Lauren and Tim will be better able to plan their purchases of ingredients. They will know which ingredients will be used more quickly based on the flavor preferences. The bar graph of Crema customers' favorite flavors is presented in Figure 1.

Name: ______________________ Date: ______________

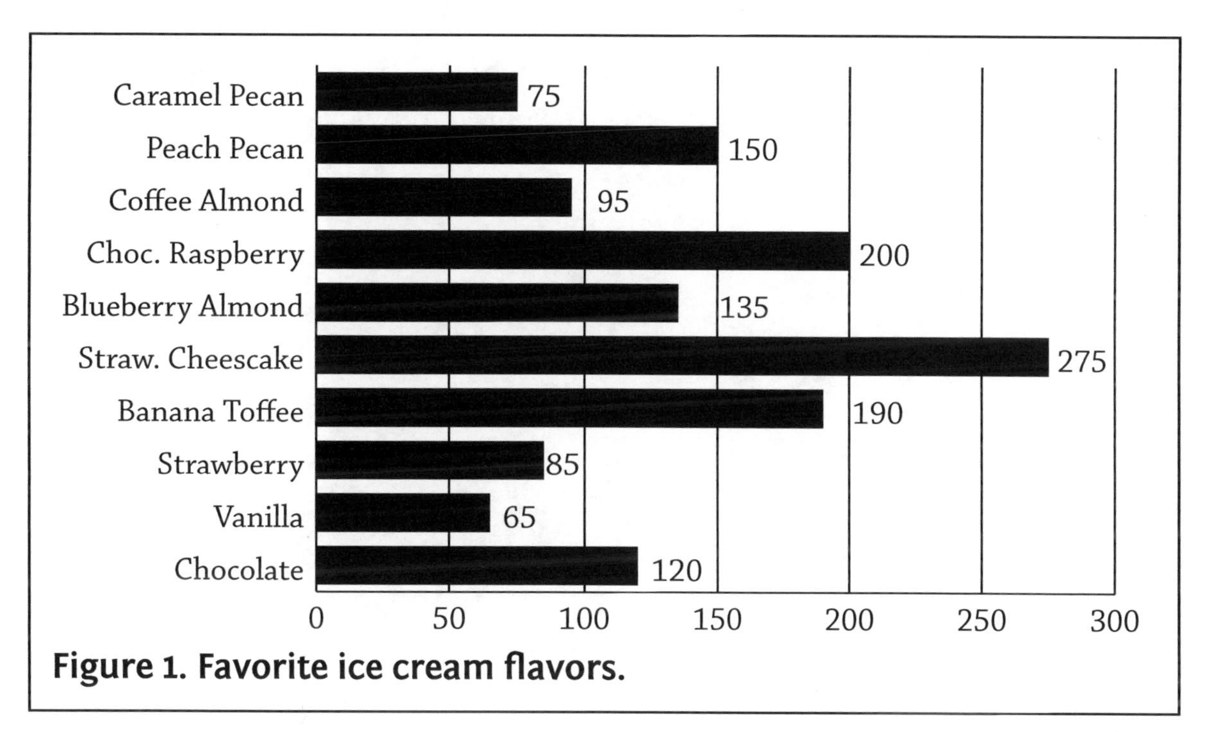

Figure 1. Favorite ice cream flavors.

After realizing how data can help them run their business more efficiently, Tim and Lauren decided to keep track of the number of customers coming to Crema on each day of the week. They were especially interested in Saturday and Sunday. They often wondered if they made or lost money by being open on the weekend. The results of their tracking are presented in Table 2.

Table 2
Number of Customers By Day

Day of the Week	Number of Customers
Monday	95
Tuesday	105
Wednesday	165
Thursday	210
Friday	275
Saturday	150
Sunday	45

Because the bar graph was helpful with comparing favorite flavors, the Crema owners decided to graph these data about customer attendance, too. However, instead of a bar graph, they chose to use a line graph. Line graphs track continuing data where one point is affected by another. With line graphs, there are points on a graph with x and y-axis coordinates. Points are then joined by a line. Line graphs often are used to track rainfall, the

Name: ______________________ Date: ______________

average daily temperature, or, in the case of Crema, the daily number of customers. The line graph they used is presented in Figure 2.

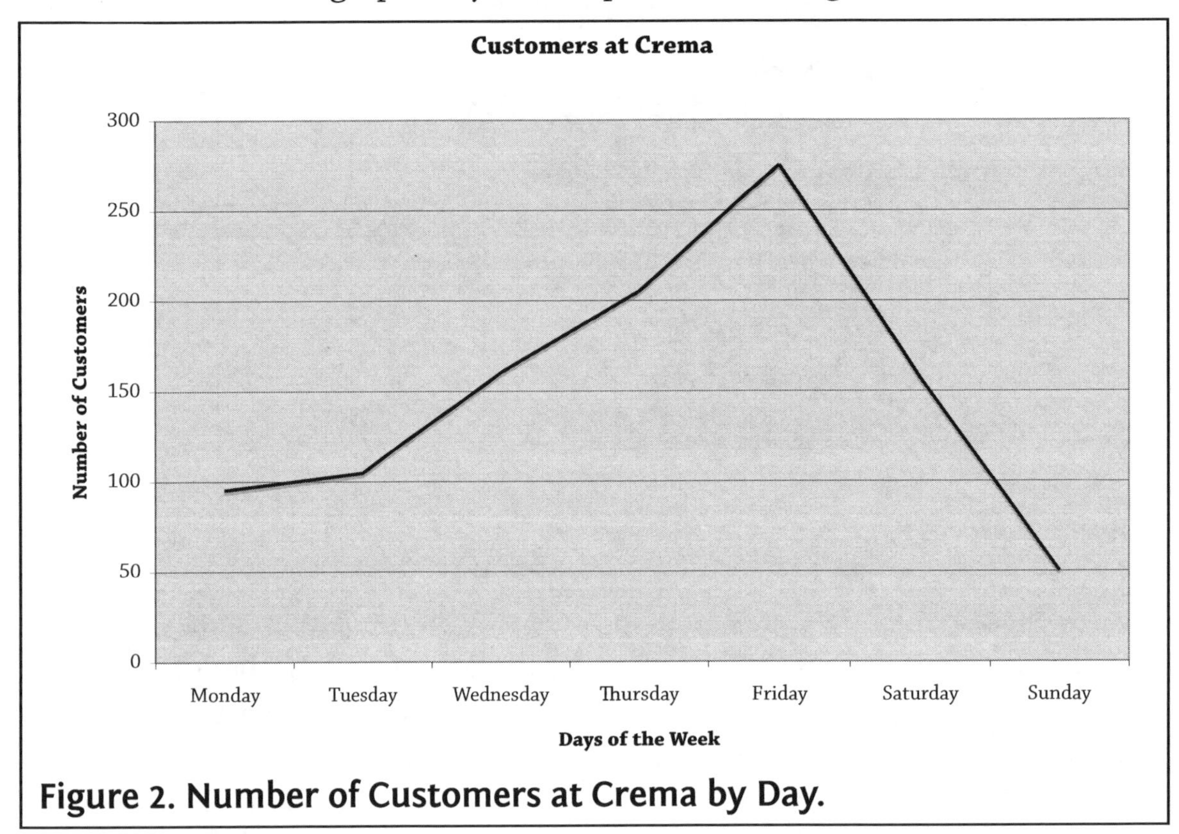

Figure 2. Number of Customers at Crema by Day.

Tim and Lauren analyzed the data to determine on what days they were most profitable. As they were thinking about money, they wondered how productive their employees were. They decided to ask their employees to keep track of how they spent their work hours. The results of this tracking are presented in Table 3.

Table 3
How Crema Employees Spend a Total Work Day (12 Hours)

Chore	Hours	Percentage of Work Day
Preparing Store to Open	1	8%
Taking Orders	3.5	30%
Preparing Orders	5	42%
Completing Transactions	1	8%
Reconciling Register	.5	4%
Closing	1	8%

Name: ______________________________ Date: ______________

The owners of Crema decided to use a circle, or pie, graph to display the data gathered from their employees. Pie graphs are particularly helpful when looking at how a part relates to a whole. In this case, Tim and Lauren wanted to see how the time spent on each chore related to the workday as a whole. The pie chart is presented in Figure 3.

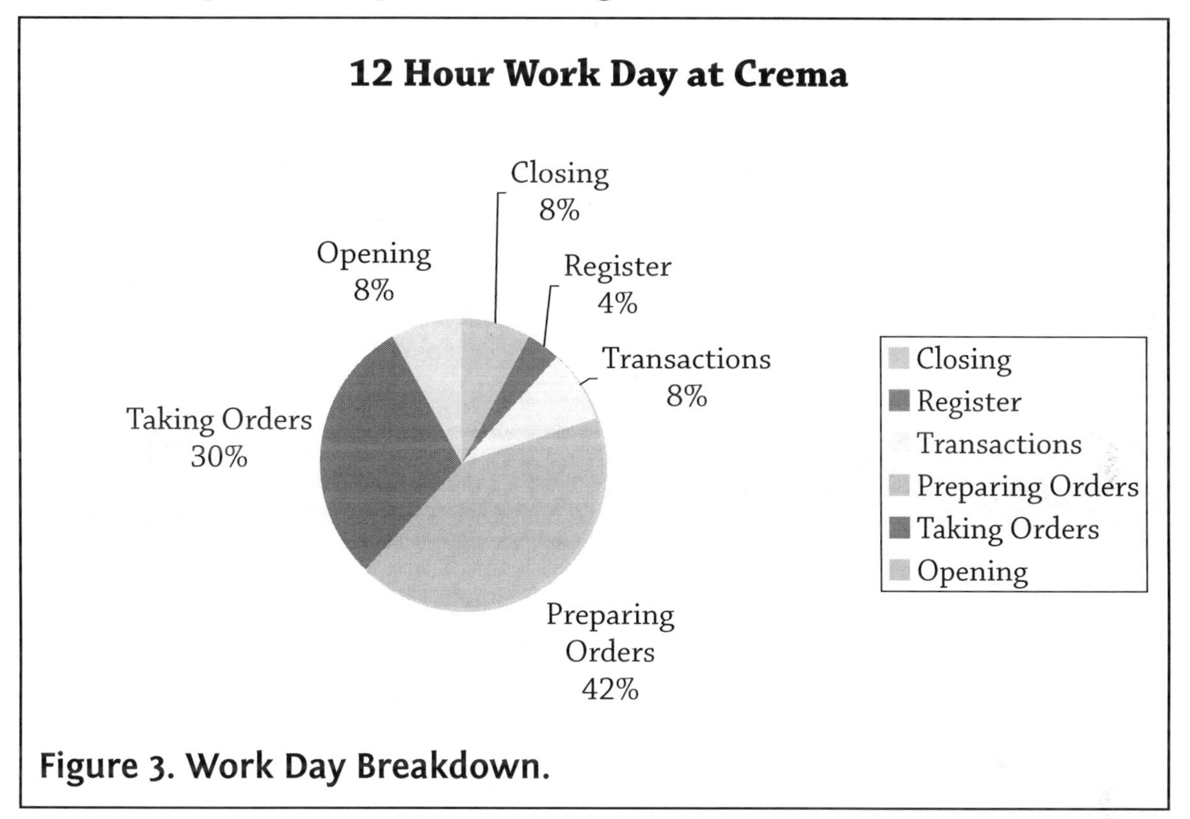

Figure 3. Work Day Breakdown.

Name: ______________________ Date: ______________

GRAPHIC ICE CREAM

B3

Generalizations

Write at least three generalizations about using graphs to represent data.

B2

Classifications

Look at your list of details. Classify your list into the categories of bar, line, or pie graphs based on which type of graph would be most appropriate for each type of data. Use the definitions from the text to make your classification decisions.

B1

Details

List 15–20 different kinds of data that are often gathered or that could be gathered.

Name: ______________________ Date: ______________

GRAPHIC ICE CREAM

Theme/Concept

C3

Why did the author title this selection "Graphic Ice Cream"? Use evidence from the text to support your answer.

Inference

C2

What inferences can you draw based on:

(a) the data and graph about customers' favorite flavors?

(b) the data and graph about daily customer counts?

(c) the data and graph about the use of employees' work hours?

Literary Elements

C1

How would you characterize the owners of Crema? Using details from the text to support your answer, describe the kind of business owners they are.

Name: ______________________________ Date: ______________

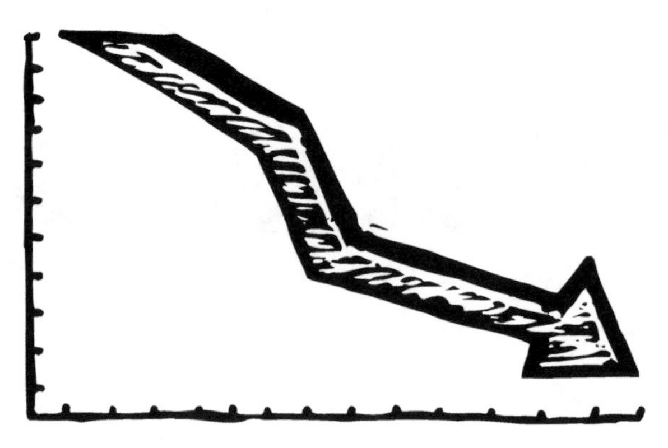

The Great Depression

The Great Depression began in the United States with the stock market crash of 1929. The Depression quickly spread throughout Europe and then the rest of the world.

Economists are divided over what caused the Great Depression. Some believe that at the end of the post-World War I building boom, consumer goods were flooding the market. The supply of goods was far exceeding demand, which caused the economic system to collapse. Others believe that it was a simple case of too many banks playing the stock market with depositors' money. A third theory contends that the Depression deepened because so many people were carrying debt before the crash, and when the crash occurred they simply stopped spending money, which crippled the capitalist market. Another theory blames the severity of the Depression on the extreme drought that struck the Midwest agricultural business during the summer of 1930. Finally, a fifth theory states that it was the collapse of foreign banks that took with it a large amount of U.S. wealth and destroyed the prospect of world trade that caused the Depression to become a Great Depression.

Regardless of the cause, the Great Depression was one of the saddest periods in U.S. history. During this time period from 1929 to 1941, Americans endured much hardship. In the Midwest, farmers experienced an intense drought that earned this agricultural area the name "Dust Bowl." During the summer of 1930, many Midwest farmers were forced to leave their lands because of dust storms that blew much of the soil away. The dust storms were caused by a failure to rotate crops and the exposure of soil by the removal of grass through plowing. With the drought, the soil dried out, became dust, and then blew away in black clouds. Much of the soil was lost in the Atlantic Ocean as it blew eastward. Many people in the Midwest suffered from dust pneumonia and malnutrition.

In other areas of the country, conditions were not any better. Unemployment rose from 5 million people without jobs in 1930 to 11 million people without jobs in 1931. A staggering 25% of Americans were unemployed. Many people lost their homes. Sadly, 20% of children were hungry and did not have proper clothing or houses. Schools had to close down because there was not enough money to keep them open. Of young people between the ages of 16 and 24, 40% of them were neither in school nor working. Children wrote letters to the First Lady, Eleanor Roosevelt, begging her to help them find food, clothing, and shelter.

After his inauguration in 1933, President Franklin D. Roosevelt passed the New Deal legislation. The New Deal restructured the economy and increased government spending to stimulate demand within the market, create jobs, and provide relief for the poor and unemployed. However, in 1937, the American economy took another nosedive that further deepened the Great Depression. During the period of the Depression, most countries experienced political upheaval that allowed dictators like Hitler, Stalin, and Mussolini to rise to power, leading to the beginning of World War II in 1939.

Supplying materials and resources for troops to protect the world against Nazi Germany stimulated economies in Europe from 1937–1939, pulling these nations out of depression. In the U.S., jobs increased, people worked overtime to make up for lost wages, and Americans agreed to rations for the first time in support of the war effort. The President pushed for a large quantity of war supplies no matter what it cost the government. In the United States, the Great Depression ended in 1941 when America entered World War II.

Name: ______________________ Date: ______________

THE GREAT DEPRESSION

Consequences and Implications

A3

What were the consequences of the Great Depression for children? Justify your answer with supporting details.

Cause and Effect

A2

What caused the end of the Great Depression in Europe? In America? Support your answer.

Sequencing

A1

List, in order, the events of the Great Depression as discussed in the text.

Name: ______________________ Date: ______________

THE GREAT DEPRESSION

B3

Generalizations

Write at least three generalizations about your life today compared to the life of a child during the Great Depression.

B2

Classifications

Study your list. Classify your details into categories. You may not have a miscellaneous or other category.

B1

Details

List at least 25 things and/or privileges that you have today that you would not have had growing up during the Great Depression.

Name: ______________________________ Date: ______________

It's Electric!

How much do you know about electricity? Electricity is the movement of charged particles in atoms. There are two kinds of charged particles: electrons have a negative charge and protons have a positive charge. Electrons and protons are constantly orbiting the nucleus of an atom. When an electromotive force is applied through an energy source such as a battery or an outlet, the electrons will jump from nucleus to nucleus along the path of the force.

The rate at which electrons move is called *current*. Current is affected by resistance, which is related to the physical properties of the material through which electrons are moving. In materials with low resistance, like copper wire, electrons are easily persuaded to leave their original nucleus and travel to the next nucleus. Copper wire is a good conductor because electrons are easily conducted, or moved, along the path of the applied electromotive force. High resistance materials, such as rubber, make it nearly impossible for electrons to move from nucleus to nucleus. Rubber does not conduct electrons along the path of applied force. Because it does not allow conduction, rubber is called an *insulator*.

Another type of electricity is static electricity. With static electricity, the electrical particles are not moving; instead a charge has built up in something, like your body after rubbing your feet on carpet. When you rub your feet on the carpet, electrons are transferred from one object to the other. One object, either your feet or the carpet, ends up with extra electrons and a negative charge while the other object is positively charged because it has more protons. For the purposes of this example, let's say your feet are negatively charged and the carpet is positively charged. Then, you touch a neutral object, such as a doorknob, and experience a shock. The shock is actually a tiny lightning bolt that occurs when the extra negatively charged electrons are transferred to the neutrally charged doorknob. The electrons in your body are attracted to the protons in the doorknob and "jump" towards them. At the same time, the electrons already in the doorknob move as far away from the new electrons as possible. In the case of electricity, opposites attract.

Ancient Greeks were familiar with static electricity. They discovered the shocking characteristics of jumping electrons when they rubbed objects on fur. However, moving electricity produced by the application of an electromotive force was not discovered until much later. Many people credit Benjamin Franklin with the discovery of electricity. While this point is debatable, it can be said without doubt that Benjamin Franklin discovered

Name: ______________________________ Date: ______________

that lightning is a form of electricity through his famous kite-flying experiment. In this experiment, Franklin tied a key to the end of a wet kite string. Then, he flew the kite during a lightning storm. When the lightning struck the key, he felt a spark on his finger and he knew that lightning was a form of electricity.

Thomas Edison is known as the inventor who was first able to capture electricity to produce light. He invented the light bulb and first demonstrated this invention on December 31, 1879 in Menlo Park, NJ. During this demonstration, he said "We will make electricity so cheap that only the rich will burn candles."

Today, electricity is everywhere. There are lights in our houses, our schools, along our streets, and in our cars. Electricity even runs through our computers, our car engines, our televisions, our radios, and our video games.

Name: ______________________ Date: ______________

IT'S ELECTRIC!

Generalizations

B3

Based on your list and your classifications, write at least three generalizations about the use of electricity.

Classifications

B2

Look at your list of examples. Classify each example into categories. You may not have a miscellaneous or other category.

Details

B1

List as many examples of the use of electricity as you can in 2 minutes. (You should have at least 25 examples.)

Name: ______________________ Date: ______________

IT'S ELECTRIC

Creative Synthesis

D3

Invent a new way to use electricity. Create an advertisement to sell your new invention to an audience of your choice (your classmates, your teachers, your parents, your city, or another audience). You may use illustrations.

Summarizing

D2

In five sentences or less, summarize what happens when you rub your feet on the carpet and then touch a doorknob.

Paraphrasing

D1

In your own words, restate what Thomas Edison meant when he said, "We will make electricity so cheap that only the rich will burn candles."

Name: ______________________ Date: ______________

The Metric System vs. the U.S. Customary System

The metric system and the U.S. customary system are both systems of measurement. So, what is the difference between them and why are there two different systems? In today's global society, wouldn't it be easier if the whole world used the same system?

Elements of the metric system date back to the reign of Louis XVI in France during the 18th century. In 1791, after the French Revolution, the metric system was adopted by the French as the official system of measurement. The goals of the new metric system were to develop a single unit for physical quantity and to create a measurement system that did not require the use of conversion factors. Specifically, all measurements of length are in meters, measurements of liquid are in liters, and measurements of weight are in grams. All three types of measurement use a common set of prefixes that are related to each other by powers of 10. For example, a decameter is 10 meters, a hectometer is 100 meters, and a kilometer is 1,000 meters. Conversely, a decimeter is $\frac{1}{10}$ of a meter, a centimeter is $\frac{1}{100}$ of a meter, and millimeter is $\frac{1}{1000}$ of a meter. There are no conversion factors required to switch among these different representations of the measurement of length. Time is the only unit of measurement that is not unified by the metric system. Time still requires conversion factors to switch among days, hours, minutes, and seconds.

The U.S. customary system can be traced back to the Roman system of measurement. It is based on the Imperial System, which was used by Great Britain until 1995. Today, the United States is the only country that has not converted to the metric system from the customary system even though the Omnibus Trade and Competitiveness Act of 1988 stated that the metric system is the preferred system for industry and trade. In the United States, the metric system is most commonly used by the military, medical field, and scientific realms. The customary system is used in most other instances. The customary system measures length in inches, feet, yards, and miles; measures general volume in cubic inches, cubic feet, and cubic yards; measures liquid volume in fluid ounces, cups, pints, quarts, and gallons; and measures weight in ounces, pounds, and tons. The customary system requires conversion factors to convert units. For example, to convert feet into yards, you must know that there are 3 feet in one yard. You then would divide the total number of feet by three to determine the

Name: ______________________ Date: ______________

total number of yards. Similarly, to convert cups into quarts, you have to know that there are 4 cups in a quart.

The chart in Figure 1 shows the conversion factors needed for the customary system compared to conversion of measurement units within the metric system.

Customary System			Metric System		
From	**Multiply by**	**To get**	**From**	**Multiply by**	**To get**
feet	12	inches	meters	1000	kilometers
pounds	16	ounces	grams	.001	milligrams
quarts	4	cups	liters	.10	deciliters

Figure 1. Converting Units in the Customary System vs. the Metric System.

Which system do you think is easier?

Name: ______________________________ Date: ______________

THE METRIC SYSTEM VS. THE U.S. CUSTOMARY SYSTEM

Consequences and Implications

A3

What are the implications of the United States being the only country that has not officially converted to the metric system? Justify your answer.

Cause and Effect

A2

What caused the French to adopt the metric system after the French Revolution? Support your answer.

Sequencing

A1

List the elements of the metric system and the U.S. customary system in the order in which they were discussed in the text.

Name: ______________________ Date: ______________

THE METRIC SYSTEM VS. THE U.S. CUSTOMARY SYSTEM

C3

Theme/Concept

Does the overall theme of the text support the use of the U.S. customary system? Why or why not?

C2

Inference

What inferences can be made from the chart in Figure 1? Support your answer with details from the text.

C1

Literary Elements

Imagine a conversation between an American and a French person about the use of the metric system vs. the customary system. Choose one character from this scenario. Describe your chosen character's point of view on this topic. Use details to support your description.

Appendix

A

Pre- and Postassessments and Exemplars

Appendix A contains the pre- and postassessment readings and answer forms, as well as a rubric for scoring the assessments. The preassessment should be administered before any work with *Jacob's Ladder* is conducted. After all readings and questions have been answered, the postassessment can be given to track student improvement on the ladder skill sets. Included in this appendix are example answers for both the pre- and postassessments. The answers are taken from student responses given during the piloting of this curriculum.

Name: ______________________________ Date: ______________

Fourth-Grade Pretest: The Old Woman and the Physician

Please read the story, "The Old Woman and the Physician," included below. Then, answer the four questions related to the story.

The Old Woman and the Physician

(Originally told by Aesop)

An old woman, having lost the use of her eyes, called in a physician to heal them and made this bargain with him in the presence of witnesses: that if he should cure her blindness, he should receive from her a sum of money; but if her infirmity remained, she should give him nothing. This agreement being made, the physician, time after time, applied his salve to her eyes, and on every visit took something away, stealing all of her property little by little. And when he had got all she had, he healed her and demanded the promised payment. The old woman, when she recovered her sight and saw none of her goods in her house, would give him nothing. The physician insisted on his claim, and as she still refused, summoned her before the judge. The old woman, standing up in the court, argued: "This man here speaks the truth in what he says; for I did promise to give him a sum of money if I should recover my sight: but if I continued blind, I was to give him nothing. Now he declares that I am healed. I on the contrary affirm that I am still blind; for when I lost the use of my eyes, I saw in my house various chattels and valuable goods: but now, though he swears I am cured of my blindness, I am not able to see a single thing in it."

1. What do you think the judge will do in this case? Why? Provide evidence from the story to defend your answer.

____

____

____

____

____

____

____

Name: ______________________________ Date: ______________

2. What does the old woman mean when she says, "but now, though he swears I am cured of my blindness, I am not able to see a single thing"? Provide evidence from the story to defend your answer.

____

____

____

____

____

____

____

3. What is the moral of this story? Give a reason why you think so.

____

____

____

____

____

____

____

4. Create a new title for this story. Give a reason why your title is better than the original title.

____

____

____

____

____

____

____

Name: ______________________ Date: ______________

Fourth-Grade Posttest: The King and the Shirt

Please read the story, "The King and the Shirt," included below. Then, answer the four questions related to the story.

The King and the Shirt

(By Leo Tolstoy)

A king once fell ill. "I will give half my kingdom to the man who can cure me," he said. All of his wise men gathered together to decide how the king could be cured. But no one knew. Only one of the wise men said what he thought would cure the king. "If you can find a happy man, take his shirt, put it on the king—and the king will be cured." The king sent his emissaries to search for a happy man. They traveled far and wide throughout his whole kingdom, but they could not find a happy man. There was no one who was completely satisfied: if a man was rich he was ailing; if he was healthy he was poor; if he was rich and healthy he had a bad wife; or if he had children they were bad—everyone had something to complain of. Finally, late one night, the king's son was passing by a poor little hut and he heard someone say: "Now, God be praised, I have finished my work, I have eaten my fill, and I can lie down and sleep! What more could I want?" The king's son rejoiced and gave orders that the man's shirt be taken and carried to the king, and that the man be given as much money as he wanted. The emissaries went in to take the man's shirt, but the happy man was so poor that he had no shirt.

1. What do you think will happen next since the happy man has no shirt? Why? Provide evidence from the story to defend your answer.

____

____

____

____

____

____

Name: ______________________________ Date: ______________

2. Why do you think the man without a shirt was happy when no one else was? Provide evidence from the story to defend your answer.

3. What is the moral of this story? Give a reason why you think so.

4. Create a new title for this story. Give a reason why your title is better than the original title.

Name: ____________________ Date: ____________

Assessment Scoring Rubric

	Points				
Question	**0**	**1**	**2**	**3**	**4**
1 Implications and Consequences (Ladder A)	Provides no response or response is inappropriate to the task demand	Limited, vague, inaccurate; rewords the prompt or copies from text	Response is accurate and makes sense but does not adequately address all components of the question or provide rationale from text	Response is accurate; answers all parts of the question; provides a rationale that justifies answer	Response is well written, specific, insightful; answers all parts of the questions, offers substantial support, and incorporates evidence from the text
2 Inference (Ladder C)	Provides no response or response is inappropriate to the task demand	Limited, vague, inaccurate; rewords the prompt or copies from text	Accurate response but literal interpretation with no support from the text	Interpretive response with limited support from the text	Insightful, interpretive, well-written response with substantial support from the text
3 Theme/ Generalization (Ladders B and C)	Provides no response or response is inappropriate to the task demand	Limited, vague, inaccurate; rewords the prompt or copies from text	Literal description of the story without explaining the theme; no reasons why	Valid, interpretive response with limited reasoning from the text	Insightful, interpretive response with substantial justification or reasoning
4 Creative Synthesis (Ladder D)	Provides no response or response is inappropriate to the task demand	Limited, vague, inaccurate; rewords the prompt or copies from text	Appropriate but literal title with no attempt to support	Interpretive title with limited reasoning or justification	Insightful title, interpretive, and extensive justification or reasoning

Example Answers

Fourth-Grade Pretest: The Old Woman and the Physician

Note. These answers are based on student responses and teacher ratings from field trials conducted by the Center for Gifted Education. The answers have not been changed from the original student response.

1. **What do you think the judge will do in this case? Why? Provide evidence from the story to defend your answer.**

   1-point responses might include:

   - Make the woman pay because she is lying.
   - I think that the judge will think that the old woman is innocent because she is still blind.
   - Tell her to get glasses or eye contacts.

   2-point responses might include:

   - I think the judge will go to the Physician's house and look for the stolen goods.
   - I think the judge will make him give her goods back to her or else be put in jail for selling her stuff.
   - The judge will not make her pay the Physician.

   3-point responses might include:

   - I think the judge will say the Physician is guilty because the woman said, "he swore he cured me but I can't see anything in my home."
   - I think the judge will say the woman won the case because the Physician stole everything the woman owned and wants more.
   - I think the judge will find the man guilty because when the old lady was going blind she could see valuable stuff but when she was cured she couldn't see valuable stuff.

   4-point responses might include:

   - I think the judge will trick the physician. The judge will say she does not have to pay until she can see her things. When the physician brings them back he will be arrested for stealing.

- I think the judge will find out the man stole little by little because before she went blind she saw various chattels but when she went blind and got better there was nothing left.
- The judge will make the Physician give back everything he took and not make the old woman pay him for curing her because he was greedy and stole her valuable goods and still demanded payment.

2. What does the old woman mean when she says, "but now, though he swears I am cured of my blindness, I am not able to see a single thing"? Provide evidence from the story to defend your answer.

1-point responses might include:

- The Physician says she is cured but she says she is not able to see a thing.
- The woman means she can't see anything because she is still blind.
- I think she means that someone tried to fix her eyes but it didn't work because she still couldn't see anything.

2-point responses might include:

- I think the old woman says that because she thinks the Physician stole all her valuable goods.
- She says that because while he was curing her he stole all of her things.
- She means she is cured but can't see her goods.

3-point responses might include:

- The old woman means that she still can't see even though she has been cured because there is nothing in her house to see.
- The old lady means that she can't see any of her possessions. That is because all of her possessions are missing.
- She can't see anything in her house because there isn't anything in her house.

4-point responses might include:

- She means she can see because the physician cured her but does not have anything to look at in her house. I think this because the story says every time the doctor gave her medicine he took something.

- She means even though she can see again, she still can't see any of her goods in her house because the Physician stole them all.
- The old woman means that she had valuable goods in her house before she went blind but when she got her sight back they were all gone so she couldn't see them anymore.

3. What is the moral of this story? Give a reason why you think so.

1-point responses might include:

- I think it is all about money.
- If you're blind, stick with it.
- The man speaks the truth.

2-point responses might include:

- The moral is the Physician stole all her goods while the woman was blind.
- The moral of this story is the Physician took all of her things.
- The moral of the story is that the old woman is blind and didn't know that her stuff was stolen and when she was cured she did not have anything.

3-point responses might include:

- The moral of the story is never steal because it is wrong.
- Don't trust someone that you don't know when you are blind, you may get something stolen.
- The moral of the story is don't promise because you could get in big trouble.

4-point responses might include:

- You should not trick someone because the person you tricked can find out everything even if they are blind, deaf, or others. My reason is that the blind woman found out the Physician stole her things and then did not pay him for curing her.
- The moral of the story is don't be greedy. The Physician stole all the old woman's stuff and tried to make her pay him and now he has to go to court and probably won't end up with anything.

- The moral of the story is to be careful who you trust, because the old woman trusted the Physician she thought was good and he stole from her.

4. Create a new title for this story. Give a reason why your title is better than the original title.

1-point responses might include:

- The Physician.
- Two People Going Blind because two people go blind.
- The Blinding Eye.

2-point responses might include:

- The Old Blind Woman and the Physician. My title is better than the other title because it talks about a blind old woman and a Physician.
- Lady and the Eye Doctor. Some people don't know what a Physician is so you can call him an eye doctor.
- The Woman and the Thief. The original title is boring.

3-point responses might include:

- Is She Blind? Because the story is trying to figure out if she's still blind.
- The Physician Bandit, because he took her stuff.
- Watch Out for the Physician. I would title it this so it could warn people about the robber physician.

4-point responses might include:

- The title I would pick is Pay If You Have To. I picked this title because she has to pay if he fixed her eyes. She promised to pay and you should keep promises.
- The Blind Woman and the Sneaky Physician. I think my title is better because it tells that the Physician took valuable things while the woman was blind. The physician was a liar and a cheat.
- The Woman and the Greedy Physician. I think my title is better than the original because the Physician stole the woman's belongings and wanted the money she said she'd give him if he cured her too.

Example Answers

Fourth-Grade Posttest: The King and the Shirt

Note. These answers are based on student responses and teacher ratings from field trials conducted by the Center for Gifted Education. The answers have not been changed from the original student response.

1. **What do you think will happen next since the happy man has no shirt? Why? Provide evidence from the story to defend your answer.**

   1-point responses might include:

   - The poor man has to have a shirt.
   - The king's men took his shirt from him.
   - He will have no shirt.

   2-point responses might include:

   - The king will die.
   - I think the king will get very sick.
   - The king will learn how to be happy.

   3-point responses might include:

   - He did not have a shirt to give to the king so the king remained uncured.
   - I think that since the happy man has no shirt they will give him one to wear for a couple weeks and then take it to the king.
   - I think since the happy man had no shirt they should find a new cure to help the king because there is no way to take a shirt from someone who doesn't have a shirt.

   4-point responses might include:

   - I think since the happy man had no shirt the king won't be cured. I know that because it says in the story "If you can find a happy man take his shirt, put it on the king—and the king will be cured" and the happy man has no shirt so the king won't be cured.

- The king will find out that you don't have to be rich to be happy since the poor man was happy without a shirt the king can be happy without a shirt too.
- I think they will keep searching for a happy man's shirt because they searched far and wide for a long time before so they'll probably keep looking.

2. Why do you think the man without a shirt was happy when no one else was? Provide evidence from the story to defend your answer.

1-point responses might include:

- He only had to get a shirt and then he could get all the money he needs.
- He was used to not having a shirt.
- I think the man was happy because the king's son said I will give you money.

2-point responses might include:

- He was happy because he could sleep.
- He was happy because he had all his work done.
- He was happy because he didn't complain.

3-point responses might include:

- He had food and a home so he was grateful for what he had.
- He had all he wanted. The man said, "What more could I want?"
- I think the poor man was happy because he didn't want anything.

4-point responses might include:

- I think the man with no shirt was happy because he was content with what he had. He said he had finished his work, eaten his fill and he could now rest.
- I think he was happy because he was thankful for what he had. It even says in the story that he was thanking God for what had happened and what he had.

- The man was happy because he didn't care that he was poor. He didn't complain like everyone else because he only cared about the important things.

3. What is the moral of this story? Give a reason why you think so.

1-point responses might include:

- What more could I want?
- The moral is always wear a shirt.
- Poor people don't always have shirts.

2-point responses might include:

- Trying to cure the king. They are trying to find a happy man with a shirt.
- The moral of the story is that the king is ill and he needs to be cured.
- The king stole shirts and he shouldn't.

3-point responses might include:

- I think the moral of this story was that it is hard to find someone who is really happy because many have many complaints and things that make them mad or sad.
- Be happy with what you already have because the man didn't have a lot.
- You don't need to be rich to be happy.

4-point responses might include:

- I think the moral of the story is to be happy with what you have. In the story the happy man was thankful for what he had. He was done working, eating and was going to go to sleep so he was happy.
- Even if you are poor and don't even have a shirt you can still be happy because the poor man with no shirt was the only man that they could find that was happy.
- You don't have to be rich to be happy. The only happy man they could find was so poor he didn't have a shirt.

4. Create a new title for this story. Give a reason why your title is better than the original title.

1-point responses might include:

- A Lot of Trouble.
- The Poor Man Gets Rich.
- The Long Journey.

2-point responses might include:

- The Ill King and the Very Poor Man because it sounds better.
- Finding a Happy Man's Shirt. The original title said, The King and the Shirt and the shirt is not a main character.
- The Never Cured King because I think it sounds exciting.

3-point responses might include:

- The Cure. Because the king is looking for a cure.
- The King's Happy Man. I think this title is better because in the story the King was sick so he searched for a happy man.
- The Man Who Was Always Happy because the story talks more about him than the ill king.

4-point responses might include:

- Be Thankful For What You Have. I think it is a better title because the story talks about all the people who should be thankful for what they have. Like the rich man who was sick and the healthy man who was poor.
- How to Be Happy. Because the story was mainly about why the happy man was happy. To be happy you should be thankful for what you have.
- The Only Happy Man. I think this is a better title because they traveled far and wide through the whole kingdom and they could only find one happy man. All the others were not totally happy.

APPENDIX

B

Record-Keeping Forms/Documents

Appendix B contains three record-keeping forms and documents:

1. *Brainstorming/Answer Sheet*: This should be given to students for completion after reading a selection so that they may jot ideas or questions about the selection they read prior to participating in discussion. The purpose of this sheet is to capture students' thoughts and ideas generated after individually reading a text. This sheet serves as a guide for student preparedness so that the student is ready to share ideas in group discussion.
2. *Reflection Page*: This form may be completed by the student after group or class discussion on the readings. The reflection page is designed as a metacognitive approach to help students reflect on their strengths and weaknesses and to promote process skills. After discussion, students use the reflection page to record new ideas that were generated by others' comments and ideas.
3. *Classroom Diagnostic Form*: This form is for teachers and is designed to aid them in keeping track of the progress and skill mastery of their students. With this chart, teachers can record student progress in relation to each ladder skill within a genre and select additional ladders and story selections based on student needs.

Brainstorming/Answer Sheet

Use this form to brainstorm thoughts and ideas about the readings and ladder questions before discussing with a partner.

Selection Title: ____________________

Circle One: **A3 B3 C3 D3**

Circle One: **A2 B2 C2 D2**

Circle One: **A1 B1 C1 D1**

Name: ______________________________ Date: ______________

Name: ________________________ Date: ____________

My Reflection on Today's Reading and Discussion

Selection Title: ______________________________

What I did well:

____

____

____

____

What I learned:

____

____

____

____

New ideas I have after discussion:

____

____

____

____

Next time I need to:

____

____

____

____

Classroom Diagnostic Form

Short Stories

Use this document to record student completion of ladder sets with the assessment of work.

0 = Needs Improvement   1 = Satisfactory   2 = Exceeds Expectations

	Androcles		Arachne and Athena		The Blue Heron		Clay Marbles, Alexei, and Me		The Fox and the Cat		The Lost Wig		Mary Poppins' Secret		The Myth of Athena		The Myth of Heracles		Theseus and the Minotaur	
Student Name	C	D	B	C	A	B	B	C	B	C	A	C	C	D	A	D	A	D	B	D

Classroom Diagnostic Form

Poetry

Use this document to record student completion of ladder sets with the assessment of work.

0 = Needs Improvement   1 = Satisfactory   2 = Exceeds Expectations

	A Bedtime Story		Cousin for Sale		Grapefruit		Lift Every Voice and Sing		My Shadow		My Sister Is a Sissy		Occupant of Room #709		Over-population		School House Is A Rockin'		Untitled	
Student Name	C	C	B	C	B	C	B	D	B	C	B	C	B	C	A	C	B	C	B	C

Classroom Diagnostic Form

Nonfiction

Use this document to record student completion of ladder sets with the assessment of work.

0 = Needs Improvement   1 = Satisfactory   2 = Exceeds Expectations

	The American Revolutionary War		The Exploration of Space		Graphic Ice Cream		The Great Depression		It's Electric		The Metric System vs. The U.S. Customary System	
Student Name	C	D	A	D	B	C	A	B	B	D	A	C

Answer Key

This key includes example answers for all ladder questions. Sample answers were generated to illustrate the skills students should be mastering. However, because the questions are open-ended and designed to promote discussion, these answers should only be used as a guide. Variations and original thought should be valued and rewarded.

Short Stories Answer Set

These are suggested answers only. Answers will vary.

Androcles

Ladder Set C

C1. Androcles is a kind, brave, and caring person. Once he realized that the lion was not going to attack him, he was not afraid of the lion anymore. Instead of running away, he cared enough to find out what was wrong with the lion. He realized the lion was another living creature that deserved care and compassion. He was kind to the lion by taking care of him.

C2. The lion did not eat Androcles because Androcles was a friend. Androcles took care of the lion's paw; without the help of Androcles the lion probably would not have survived because it would have been attacked by an enemy or killed by an infection from the wound. I was not surprised the lion spared Androcles because animals often are as loyal as or more loyal than people.

C3. Answers will vary. An example might be, "Be kind to others and they will be kind to you" because Androcles helped the lion who returned the favor by not eating him.

Ladder Set D

D1. The Lion recognized Androcles as the person who helped him when his paw was hurt. He knew he could not hurt someone who had been so kind to him. He decided he would rather go hungry than to harm a friend. The emperor was so impressed that he demanded Androcles tell him why the lion did not eat him. The emperor was amazed at the friendship and decided to free both Androcles and the lion.

D2. You never know when a kindness toward another will be repaid. (Support: Androcles didn't foresee a situation for the lion to repay the favor, but when such a situation did arise, the lion was quick to treat Androcles as he had been treated.)

D3. Answers will vary. The fable should be short, have a moral, and be related to the main idea identified by the student in the answer to D2.

Arachne and Athena

Ladder Set B

B1. Answers will vary. Some examples might include: She will not be able to walk around town without fear of getting stepped on; she will not be able to sell her cloth; she will not be able to weave cloth, only webs; she will not be able to talk; she will have to eat flies.

B2. Answers will vary. Some examples using the list above might include: relationships with others, livelihood, or lifestyle.

B3. Answers will vary. An example using the list and categories above might be: "Change can be positive or negative."

Ladder Set C

C1.

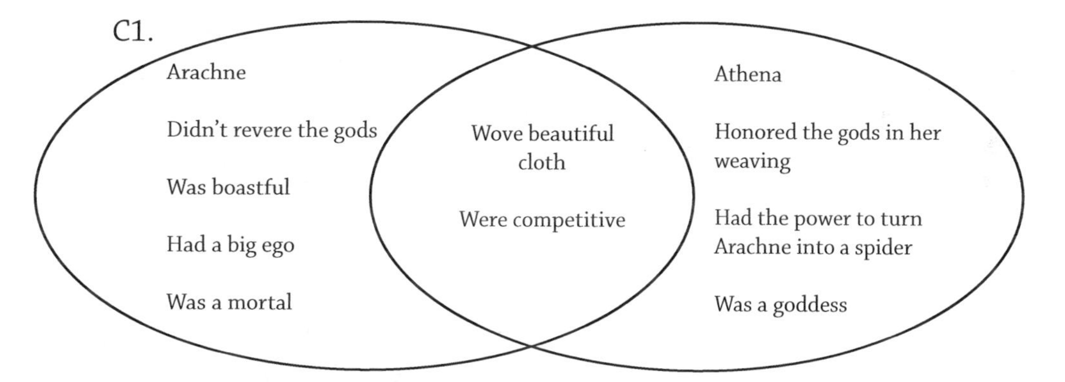

C2. Arachne tried to outweave Athena because she thought she was a better weaver and she wanted to prove it. Also, Arachne did not respect the gods and goddesses, including Athena. Arachne thought she could prove the gods and goddesses were no different or better than mortals.

C3. We learn that we should not be egotistical. We should not think we are better at a skill than everyone else, but should appreciate everyone's talents.

The Blue Heron

Ladder Set A

A1. 1. Jon shot the heron like his father wanted; 2. Jon realized the heron was a female and probably left behind a chick; 3. Jon found the chick and took care of it; 4. Jon's father found out and shot Jon while trying to shoot the chick; 5. Jon's father realizes that his son should be able to have his own set of values even if they are different than his.

A2. Jon gets a camera for his birthday because his father has realized that Jon does not want the same things as he does out of life. His father realizes that Jon never wanted to shoot birds; he only did so to please his father. The camera sends an unspoken message to Jon that being true to himself will make his father proud.

A3.

a.) Jon would not have realized the heron had a chick, would not have brought the chick to the barn, would not have gotten shot while trying to protect the chick, and his father would not have realized Jon's true feelings about birds.

b.) Jon's father would have been consumed with guilt for the rest of his life and Jon never would have experienced full acceptance from his father.

c.) Jon's father probably would have been mad and demanded Jon change his beliefs. Or, Jon's father might have understood his son's wishes not to hunt and no one would have gotten hurt.

d.) Jon would have difficulty forgiving his father for shooting the innocent bird and would have disliked hunting even more.

Ladder Set B

B1. Answers will vary. Some examples might include: Jon's father wanted to kill the heron because he could make a lot of money from the bird's body, especially if the bird's feathers were not marred and he could stuff it; this money would then allow him to support his family. Jon did not want to kill the heron because he thought it was more beautiful in its natural habitat than stuffed; he also believes all living things should be allowed to live in peace.

B2. Answers will vary. Examples based on the above reasons might include: Positive—Jon thinks birds should live in peace; birds are beautiful in their natural habitats; Jon's father wanted to support his family; Negative—Birds should die just for money.

B3. Answers will vary. Examples based on the above list and categories might include:

a.) Hunting should be taken seriously because something or someone must pay a price.

b.) People who hunt do not respect living creatures.

c.) People who don't like hunting have a greater appreciation for living creatures.

Clay Marbles, Aleksei, and Me

Ladder Set B

B1. Answers will vary. Some examples might include:

- narrator—reminiscent, a servant, a child, alone, protective, mischievous
- Rasputin—filthy, frightening, a fraud, ugly, smelled bad
- Fabergé—loved, artist, elegant, interesting, doting.

B2.

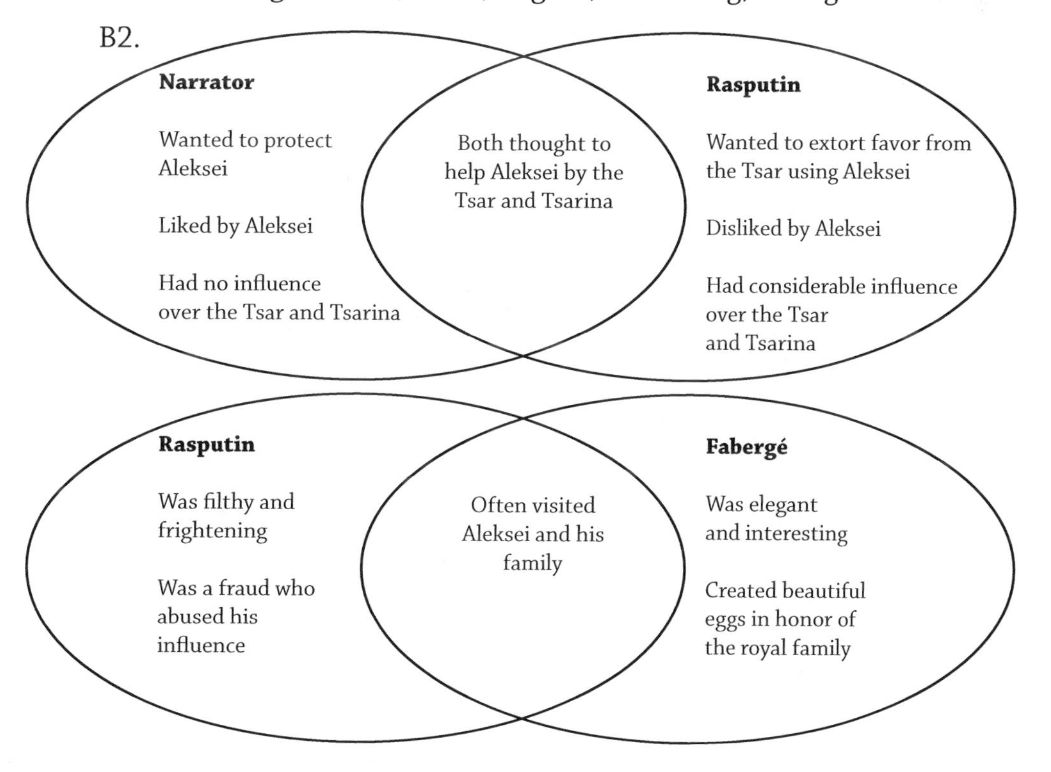

B3. Answers will vary. An example using the Venn diagrams above might be, "The narrator put the safety of Aleksei above her own."

Ladder Set C

C1. Aleksei was a sick young boy who had a loyal, devoted friend in the form of a young servant girl (support: the story is told from the young servant girl's point of view and as a fond memory of days gone by). His family cared about him, but also had a difficult time seeing beyond his illness (support: they allowed the young servant girl to play with him, but they also allowed Rasputin, whom Aleksei didn't like, to visit just because Rasputin claimed he could heal Aleksei).

C2. Yes, she would. She is remembering her time with Aleksei and his family as perhaps the fondest moments in her life. She worries that Aleksei is in danger and would very much like to be near him again to serve as his protector.

C3. Family, love, friendship, loyalty, faith

The Fox and the Cat

Ladder Set B

B1. Answers will vary. Some examples might include: running from his enemies, hiding, chasing the enemies, using a weapon, using martial arts, or distracting his enemies.

B2. Answers will vary. Some example categories based on the list above might include: escape by physical outmaneuvering, escape by tactical outmaneuvering, or escape by stealth.

B3. Answers will vary. An example based on the list and categories above might be: "One tried and true, good way of escape is better than multiple mediocre options."

Ladder Set C

C1.

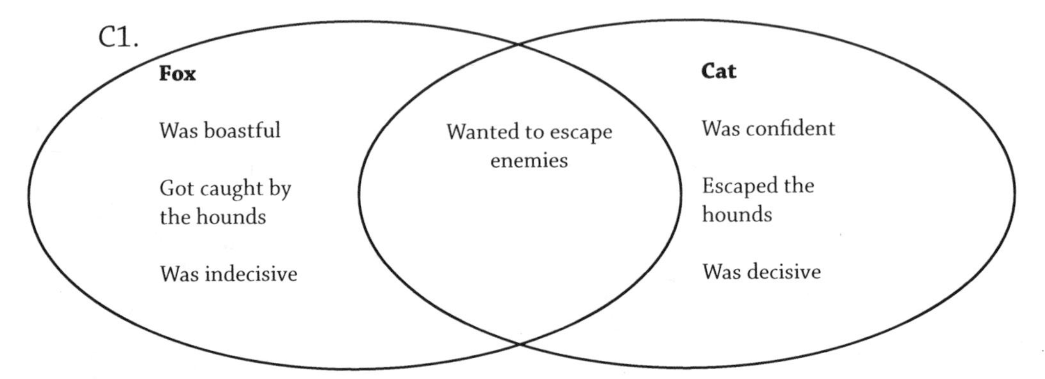

C2. The fox would be the kind of person who always talks about everything he can do, but when an actual situation arises he is unable to do anything at all. The cat would be the kind of person who doesn't say much but always comes through in a crucial situation. The evidence in the text to support my inferences are the fox's and the cat's words at the beginning of the fable, as well as the fact that the fox got caught and the cat did not.

C3.

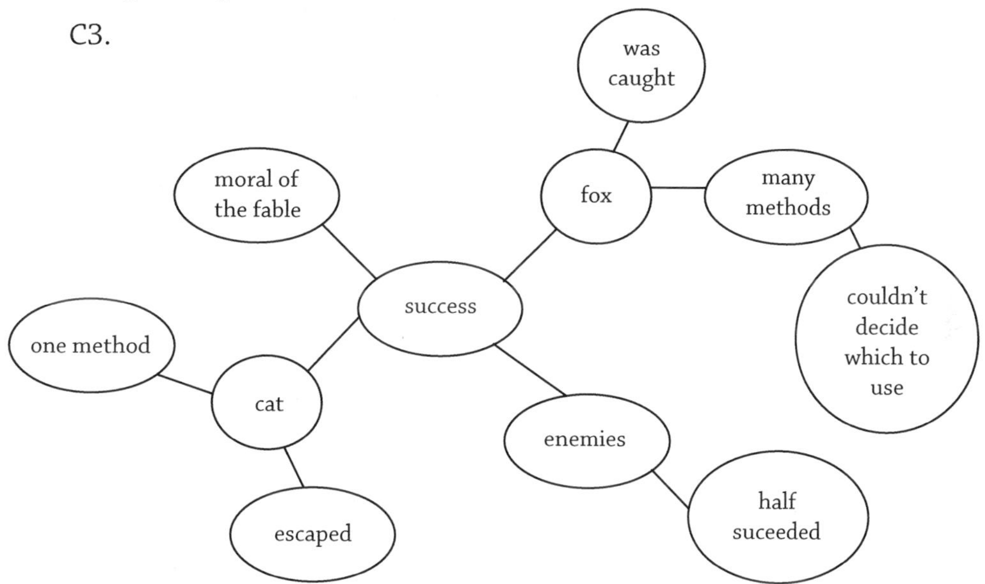

The Lost Wig

Ladder Set A

A1. 1. The lion, who was wearing a wig, was walking down the street; 2. The lion saw a pretty tiger; 3. The lion bowed to the tiger; 4. The lion's wig flew off; 5. The lion made a funny comment rather than being embarrassed.

A2. The lion bowed because he was trying to make a good impression on the tiger. The effect of his action was for his wig to fly off and the tiger to know that he did not have a real mane.

A3. I think the tiger will laugh and begin a conversation with the lion. I think this will happen because the lion did not run off embarrassed, but instead acknowledged what happened with his wig. His comment let the lady tiger know that he did not take himself too seriously.

Ladder Set C

C1. Answers will vary. Students should include both physical and personality characteristics of the lion. His most important characteristics might include being able to laugh at himself because he did not get upset when his wig flew off; being vain and feeling he had to wear a wig in the first place; and wanting the lady tiger to like him because this desire caused him to bow, which led to his wig being blown off by the wind

C2. He expected the lady tiger to be flattered and impressed by his manners. The text says he wanted to "make an impression," and by smiling and bowing it can be inferred that he wanted to make a good impression.

C3. Answers will vary. An example might be, "Don't take your appearance too seriously." If the lion had gotten upset instead of making a joke about the way he looked without his wig, the atmosphere between the lion and the tiger would have been awkward.

Mary Poppins' Secret

Ladder Set C

C1.

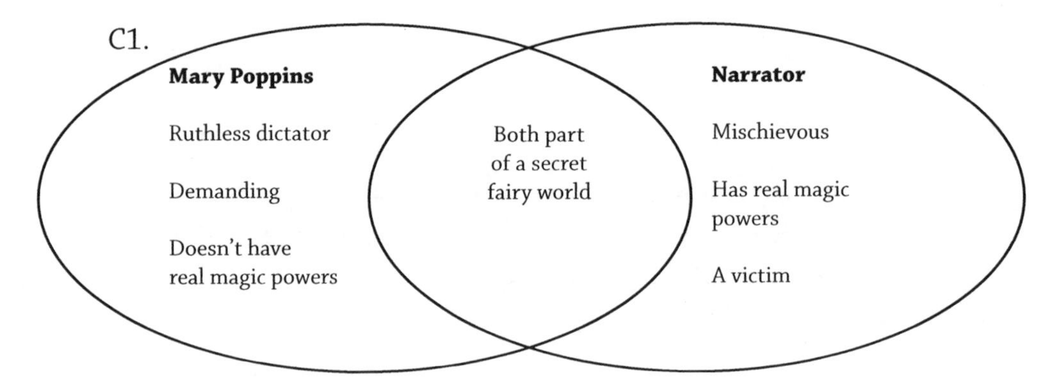

C2. The narrator provides a memo from Mary Poppins with a list of chores the narrator was to complete for her. In parentheses, the narrator explains how she used her magic to perform these chores and make them look as if Mary was doing them. Based on this evidence, Mary Poppins is a fraud because she didn't really do any of the things she claimed to do.

C3. The narrator shared the memo with the world because she wanted to expose Mary Poppins as a fraud. She wants to share the idea that people should not take credit for accomplishments they do not do themselves.

Ladder Set D

D1. Because of everything the narrator did for Mary Poppins, Mary became famous. Someone wrote a book about her that became very popular with parents and children alike. The narrator feels a bit cheated; all she wanted was recognition and a thank you from Mary Poppins acknowledging the fact that Mary could not have achieved her fame without the help of the fairy narrator. However, the narrator could not write a book about her deeds because of the Fairyland rules.

D2. The main idea of the story is to warn people against taking credit for things they do not do because, eventually, the truth will be discovered. Mary used the narrator to make herself look good, and now, because the narrator's journal was discovered, the whole world will know she is a fraud.

D3. Answers will vary. Students should use the memo from the story as a model and should include information that relates to the main idea of Mary using the narrator to achieve misplaced fame.

The Myth of Athena

Ladder Set A

A1. 1. Zeus was threatened by the possibility of being overthrown by his child; 2. Zeus swallowed his pregnant wife, Metis; 3. Athena emerged from Zeus's split skull; 4. Athena became the goddess of wisdom and the goddess of war; 5. Athena was revered by the Greeks and was attributed with providing mankind all of the necessary knowledge for a civilization

A2. Athena had so much wisdom because she possessed the combined wisdom of Zeus and Metis. When Zeus swallowed Metis, he absorbed her wisdom and combined it with his own. When Athena emerged from Zeus's skull, after Zeus had had a terrible headache, she had "inherited" the wisdom of both her parents.

A3. Wagon: We would not have transportation today. The wagon preceded the car as a mode of transportation. If mankind had never realized the increased efficiency of moving goods with a wagon compared to on foot, then we would all still be transporting goods by foot.

Plough: We would have more difficulty providing enough food for the world's population. The plough made farming faster and easier, thereby making it possible for one farmer to produce more crops, and provide more food to more people.

Shipbuilding: We would not know anything about the rest of the world. America would probably have not been found. Ships enabled explorers and traders to sail to far away lands. Without ships we would only be able to explore areas that were connected by land.

Ladder Set D

D1. Athena was revered by the Greeks for her knowledge about how to advance mankind and make civilizations more efficient, as well as for her ability to plan war strategies, which led to successful outcomes for the Greeks.

D2. Athena's wisdom would have helped her as the goddess of war because she would have immense knowledge about different types of wars, tactics, and strategies. She also would be better able to understand the motives of the enemies through her knowledge of people.

D3. Answers will vary. Stories should refer to wisdom or knowledge about strategy or tactics as it applies to the winning of a war or series of wars.

The Myth of Heracles (Hercules)

Ladder Set A

A1. 1. Heracles strangled two serpents in his crib; 2. Heracles killed his children in an anger-induced frenzy; 3. Heracles was sentenced to complete 12 labors to atone for his wrongdoing; 4. He completed all of the labors without being harmed; 5. Heracles died from wearing a tunic tainted by poison.

A2. Heracles had to complete the 12 labors because he killed his children. He spent nearly his entire life completing the tasks; did not get to spend time with his wife or use his strength to support his family. The labors were all-consuming.

A3. Heracles' manner of death was ironic because he had survived many more incidences that were far more dangerous than getting dressed. He did not know the tunic was full of poison because he could not see it. Therefore, he could defeat the enemies he could see, but not those that were disguised.

Ladder Set D

D1. Answers will vary. One may include: Heracles was forced to fight one of the most dangerous mythological creatures ever to have lived—the Hydra. The Hydra had many different heads that would regrow and double if they were cut off. If any of Hydra's heads were to breathe on Heracles, he would have died instantly. However, Heracles figured out the Hydra's heads could not grow back if the he was able to burn the wound he inflicted on the Hydra immediately after cutting off one of its heads. Heracles asked his nephew to help him; together they defeated the mighty Hydra.

D2. Heracles, who possessed superhuman strength, was able to defeat a series of mythical creatures and complete a series of arduous tasks to atone for the murder of his children. Nearly his whole life was spent in the completion of these tasks. Ironically, he died from an action much less dangerous than many he had completed before.

D3. Answers will vary. Students should include all of the elements of a myth, such as a god or goddess and a lesson to be learned. The character in the students' myths should have to atone for some crime he or she committed.

Theseus and the Minotaur

Ladder Set B

B1. Answers will vary. Some examples related to the story might include: by taking the place of the woman's son; by trusting Ariadne's directions regarding the labyrinth; by attacking the Minotaur; by going into the Labyrinth alone; by escaping King Minos' men; by not going back for Ariadne.

B2. Answers will vary. Some categories based on the above examples might be physical bravery, emotional bravery, and desire to help others.

B3. Answers will vary. An example based on the above categories and list might be, "Bravery is not just about doing dangerous physical actions."

Ladder Set D

D1. While Theseus was on Crete, he was in a hurry to find and slay the Minotaur without King Minos figuring out what he was doing. The beautiful daughter of King Minos, Ariadne, helped him by telling him the secrets of the labyrinth and giving him some gold thread to trail behind him. Theseus trusted Ariadne, even though he didn't know here very well. He found the Minotaur, killed it, and then found his way out of the labyrinth by following the trail of gold thread. Then, he rushed to his ship to get away from Crete before King Minos' soldiers could catch him.

D2. King Minos was mistreating the young people of Athens, and Theseus thought the cruelty should stop. As heir to the throne, Theseus decided it was his responsibility to rid Athens of the Minotaur menace. He killed the Minotaur and escaped King Minos' men. But, in the excitement of the moment, Theseus forgot to change his black sail to a white sail, which caused his father to jump off a cliff in grief for his lost son. Theseus won the respect of Athens and the love of Ariadne, but he lost his father.

D3. Answers will vary. Myth should be told from the point of view of one of the characters and should include all of the major events such as Theseus taking the place of the boy, slaying the Minotaur, and escaping King Minos' men.

Poetry Answer Set

These are suggested answers only. Answers will vary.

A Bedtime Story

Ladder Set C1

C1. The poem is written from the point of view of the witch's child. The second line makes this clear with the phrase, "says witch's child."

C2. Students may infer that the witch's child likes ideas that we would normally think of as being scary. The witch's child also likes to hear stories before he or she goes to bed. Students may cite the last two lines to support these inferences.

C3. The titles will vary. There should be an acceptable explanation for the choice such as "These are all poems that a witch's child might like," or "These are all poems that would be read by monsters." The poem titles will reflect the generalization the student makes to explain his or her choices.

Ladder Set C2

C1. Answers will vary, but should mention the wild beasts, shrieking/groaning ghosts, rattling skeleton, creep/crawly monsters.

C2. Students should infer that the witch's child likes to be told bedtime stories. The child also likes the creatures mentioned in the poem and thinks of these creatures as comforting.

C3. Answers will vary, although each poem should begin: "'Tell me a story,' says the ________'s child," and should continue for 12 lines. The poem should have characters appropriate to the "teller" of the poem, and a final line that helps the reader understand the teller's point of view.

Cousin for Sale

Ladder Set B

B1. Each student should list characteristics that include: whiny, bratty, wets the bed, copies people, bothers people, starts pillow fights, clumsy, stupid, bad manners, scared of dogs, falls off bike, cries, wants to play store, selfish, wants to play dress-up, wants to hear a bedtime story, messy, disgusting, makes messes, picks up worms, wants cookies, drools, gets dirty, obnoxious, loud, likes Barney, scared of E.T.

B2. The list should be sorted and classified by a system that the student can defend. Answers will vary, but might include groups such as "Attitude: whiny, bratty, cries; Actions: wets the bed, copies people, bothers people, pillow fights, falls off bike, wants to play store, makes messes, picks up worms, wants cookies, drools, gets dirty," and so on.

B3. Answers will vary, but should use the titles from the groups in B2. Examples might be: "The cousin's attitude is annoying."

Ladder Set C

C1. The student should create a Venn Diagram to compare and contrast the cousin in the poem with a child he or she knows. Label one circle with the name of the child he or she knows and the other circle with "The cousin." They list characteristics that are different in the outside parts of the circles and characteristics that are the same in the overlapping part of the circle.

C2. Answers will vary; the students should infer that the author feels exasperated, frustrated, annoyed, irritated, aggravated, upset, angry, bothered, troubled, perturbed, and so forth. (You might point the students to the Internet to look for lists of feeling words.) They should be able to explain reasons for these feelings, using text from the poem. For example, the narrator feels annoyed because her cousin wants to follow her around everywhere.

C3. Answers will vary. Each student should create a poem from the cousin's point of view that is at least 16 lines long.

Grapefruit

Ladder Set B

B1. Characteristics should include: orb (round), sunny (may say yellow), full of light, broad, square, tart, sweet, mellow mask (peel), needs sunshine, and so forth.

B2. The answers can be sorted in any logical way. This is only an example:

Sight	Sound	Feel	Taste	Smell
orb		mellow mask	tart	
sunny		needs sun	sweet	
full of light				
broad				
square				

B3. Students should examine their categories from B2 and make generalizations about adjectives such as the following: describing words help the reader better understand what the author is writing about and describing words help the author create a word picture for the reader. When people picture things in their minds they might be able to better understand the reading. For the second question students should conclude that there is a balance of using too many or too few adjectives. Writers need to include enough describing words to help the reader create images in their mind but using too many may confuse the reader or make the reader lose track of the important points in the story.

Ladder Set C

C1. Examples of personification may include the grapefruit is cheerful; wearing a yellow mask; keeping its secret.

C2. Answers may vary, but may include: mellow orb (it is round); sunny and cheerful (sunny, yellow); full of light (light, the sunshine makes it); broad and square (it is large); sliced in half like a magician's stunt (we usually cut them in half to eat them); tart, yet slightly sweet (sweet and sour taste); concealed inside a mellow mask (thick peel); a sister to a coconut (similar size and shape to a coconut); soaking up the sun (they need sun to develop); keeping its secret sealed inside to share with everyone (they must be opened in order to eat the fruit).

C3. Answers will vary; students should select an object, brainstorm ways to describe that object, and use those brainstormed words in a poem similar to "Grapefruit." Look for personification in their poems. As a teacher, you may need to brainstorm ways to personify an object as a class before allowing students to create their own personification poems.

Lift Every Voice and Sing

Ladder Set B

B1. Examples:

Now	**Past**
the present	the dark
come to the place	trod
treading	had died
	have come
	has brought us

B2. Examples:

Sorrow	**Joy**
dark past	sing
stony road	heavens ring
bitter	rejoicing
chastening rod	full of faith
hope unborn had died	hope
weary feet	rising sun
tears	new day
blood of the slaughtered	victory
gloomy past	steady beat
	bright star

B3. Answers will vary, but might include: the past was full of sadness and sorrow; the present is more joyful.

Ladder Set D

D1. Answers will vary, but might include:
  1. We walked on a stony road.
  2. The rod that beat us was unpleasant.
  3. Those were the days when we had no hope.
  4. But we kept going
  5. Even though we were tired
  6. Haven't we come to the place our fathers longed for?
  7. There has been much sadness.
  8. There have been people killed and wounded.
  9. The past was gloomy.
  10. Now we are here
  11. In a place where life is good.

D2. Answers will vary. Students should get the idea that it has taken a long time and much hard work to move from a society of slavery to a society of equality.

D3. Answers will vary. Students will create a new poem with 10 lines. The first and last line will be the same as the first and last lines of the first stanza of "Lift Every Voice and Sing."

My Shadow

Ladder Set B

B1. Answers will vary, but might include: like the little boy; likes to grow; doesn't know how to play; cowardly; lazy

B2. Answers will vary. Students should create lists of the words and phrases from activity 1 and create a title for each list.

B3. Answers will vary, but might include: shadows do whatever the person does; shadows don't know how to play.

Ladder Set C

C1. He describes his shadow as a friend, but an annoying friend.

C2.

Like the little boy	He is similar to the little boy
Jumps	He does what the boy does (copies)
Grows quickly	Not like a regular child
Makes a fool of the little boy	Makes fun
Stays too close	Not brave
Sleepy head	Lazy

C3. Answers will vary. The author wants the reader to know that a child can have a playmate and be creative even when he is alone.

My Sister Is a Sissy

Ladder Set B

B1. Answers will vary. Students will list things the sister is afraid of. They will list things they are afraid of. They will compare and contrast the two lists. Their lists might look like the following:

Sister	Me
Dogs	
Cats	
Shadows of bats	
Furry things	
Feathery things	
Big, ugly people	
Scaly things	

B2. Answers will vary. The student will categorize their list of fears and label each category with a describing word.

B3. Answers will vary. Students may generalize that everyone is afraid of something. Some fears are real and some are unfounded. They also may note that fear is relative to an individual

Ladder Set C

C1. Alliteration appears in the following phrases: Sister is a sissy; she shivers at the shadows; fur and fluffy feathers; for her fears . . . fur; she is scared

C2. Answers will vary. Students should explain their choice and use evidence from the poem to explain their answer.

C3. Answers will vary. Students will create a new title. The new title should focus on a major idea of the poem.

Occupant of Room #709

Ladder Set B

B1. Answers will vary. The character is old. She enjoyed dancing when she was young. She can no longer dance. She misses dancing.

B2. Answers will vary. Some students may infer that the woman is in a nursing home.

B3. Answers will vary. Students should make two generalizations. Example: The woman misses dancing. The woman wishes she were young again.

Ladder Set C

C1. The paragraph should say that in the past, the woman was young and active; she loved to dance. In the present, she is old and unable to dance; but she remembers when she was young.

C2. Answers will vary. Students may say that the poem is sad because the woman can't do what she used to do. Examples of words from the poem might be: stares off; feet don't move.

C3. Answers will vary. Students may say that one important idea is that life changes. We all age and our abilities change when we age.

Overpopulation

Ladder Set C

A1. The author suggests riding your bike instead of driving your car and using less electricity.

A2. Diagrams will vary. See the first half of the poem for evidence. Possible effects could include: less animal diversity, higher temperatures, less space for everyone.

A3. Student poems will vary. Make sure the students include the effects of their issue, as well as solutions to solve the issue. Also, make sure the poem flows from idea to idea without being forced due to the beginning letter of each line.

Ladder Set C

C1. The author characterizes the earth as cramped and destructive. In the first two lines of the poem that author states the world population is increasing. Because so many people are living on earth, we are taking up all the space and leaving no space for other animals. We are destroying animals' habitats and our own.

C2. In the last line of the poem the author states that everyone needs to care about the Earth. When the author says "Zest about saving the world should be spread around" he means that everyone should take responsibility for this problem because we are all part of the problem so we should all try to help.

C3. Letters will vary. Students' work should include details regarding destruction of habitats and environmental conditions that hurt plants and animals. Students can be creative with this piece as they are supposed to be taking the point of view of an animal or plant.

School House Is A Rockin'

Ladder Set B

B1. Actions include: Principal is knocking on the door; teachers are dancing; chairs (personification) are moving around; children are jiggling; desks (personification) are wiggling; schoolhouse is rocking (dancing); phone is ringing; parents are worrying; and secretary is pouring tea.

B2. Answers will vary. Students should put the answers from Activity B1 into categories and make appropriate titles for each group.

B3. Answers will vary. Students should write three generalizations about their categories from Activity B2.

Ladder Set C

C1. Examples of repetition include: Schoolhouse is a rockin'; Teachers are a dancin'; Chairs are a prancin'; Principal is a knockin'.

C2. Answers will vary. Students may say that the author wanted the reader to laugh because it is funny. Words: verbs ending in in' instead of ing, such as jigglin' and wigglin.'

C3. Answers will vary. Students may say that school is fun. They may say that the secretary is the only one who doesn't have fun.

Untitled

Ladder Set B

B1. Answers will vary. Students will chose an object and list human characteristics for the object.

B2. Answers will vary. Students will create two T-charts. They will use one to list phrases from the poem and characteristics of real seeds that may have prompted the author to use those phrases. They will use the other T-chart to list phrases they created in Activity B1 and characteristics of the real object that prompted them to use those phrases.

B3. Answers will vary. Be sure students apply personification appropriately to their selected object.

Ladder Set C

C1. dancing; she knew she wouldn't be a weed; danced; landed; became

C2. The seed is happy because she would never be a weed; she didn't need or want anything; she was dancing. Students also should be able to articulate how personification provides images people can connect with and makes writing more realistic and meaningful. In this poem, if the seed had not been given human characteristics, the mood of the poem may have been less happy and lighthearted. However, the mood could have been darkened if more negative characteristics were used.

C3. Answers will vary.

Nonfiction Answer Set

These are suggested answers only. Answers will vary.

The American Revolution

Ladder Set C

C1. Answers will vary. Check students' answers for consistency with the type of colonist they choose. For example, if they choose to write from the point of view of a Patriot, then the description of the character should include support of the war.

C2. Answers will vary. Possible answers might include: the French became allies with the Americans because they wanted another chance to fight Britain; they disliked Britain so much that they would ally themselves with anyone who was fighting against Britain; they supported freedom for America; and so forth.

C3. Answers will vary. Possible answers might include: liberty, freedom, independence, right to form their own government, democracy, and so forth.

Ladder Set D

D1. Answers will vary. Students must restate the quotations and not merely change a few words.

D2. Answers will vary. Students should include important events such as taxation without representation, the Boston Massacre, the desire for a democratic government, and so forth.

D3. Answers will vary. Check students' answers for consistency and accuracy with respect to their chosen point of view.

The Exploration of Space

Ladder Set A

A1. Oct. 4, 1957, Soviet Union launched Sputnik; April 12, 1961, Yuri Gagarin, Soviet cosmonaut, became the first human to travel into space; December 1968, Apollo 8 orbited the moon 10 times; July

20, 1969, Neil Armstrong became the first astronaut to walk on the moon

A2. When the space shuttle is launching, the Earth's gravitational pull makes it difficult for the spacecraft to move. The spacecraft must use a lot of rocket-fueled power to break the pull of gravity. After the spacecraft reenters the atmosphere, Earth's gravitational pull causes it to start falling back to Earth.

A3. Answers will vary. Students should mention that space exploration has allowed scientists to learn a lot about the universe beyond Earth. They also should provide examples from the text and/or from prior knowledge.

Ladder Set D

D1. Answers will vary. Students must restate the quotation, not merely change a few words.

D2. Answers will vary. Students should include the important elements of space exploration, such as manned shuttles, satellites, robots, and MMUs.

D3. Answers will vary. Evaluate student responses based on creativity, specificity, and accuracy.

Graphic Ice Cream

Ladder Set B

B1. Answers will vary. Check students' answers to ensure they are accurate in terms of listing data that can be collected. Examples include: classmates' favorite books, rainfall, snowfall, grades on tests, number of students buying lunch each day, growth rate of plants, and so forth.

B2. Answers will vary based on details on students' lists. Details in each category should match the definitions of bar, line, and pie graphs found in the text.

B3. Answers will vary. Generalizations should be broad, overarching statements about the use of graphs to represent data.

Ladder Set C

C1. Answers will vary. Possible answers might include: responsible; eager to make their business as efficient as possible; good managers; interested in making money; considerate of their customers; and so forth.

C2. Answers will vary. Possible answers might include:

a.) The customers' favorite flavor is strawberry cheesecake; their least favorite flavor is vanilla; they should stock plenty of strawberries and pecans.

b.) The day with the most customers is Friday; the day with the least customers is Sunday; the owners might be losing money by staying open on Sunday.

c.) The employees spend most of their time preparing orders; they spend the least amount of time reconciling the register; and the employees are good workers who use their time wisely.

C3. Answers will vary. Students should include a statement about graphs being a description of the kind of data used by the ice cream store owners to analyze the efficiency and effectiveness of their business.

The Great Depression

Ladder Set A

A1. Stock market crash of 1929; drought in the Midwest during the summer of 1930; unemployment in 1930 and 1931; inauguration of FDR in 1933; downturn in the economy in 1937; beginning of WWII in 1939; upswing in European economies from 1937–1939; end of the Great Depression/U.S. enters WWII in 1941.

A2. The end of the Great Depression in Europe was caused by the rearmament of troops to protect the world against Nazi Germany; the end of the Great Depression in America was caused by the creation of jobs to produce large amounts of war supplies and rations to support the war effort as the U.S. began fighting in WWII.

A3. Answers will vary. Possible answers might include: They couldn't go to school to get an education which would lead to better jobs in the future; they did not have homes to live in and therefore did not enjoy the security that children today experience; they were often hungry and malnourished; they may not have grown as well as they should because they didn't have enough to eat and may, therefore, have shortened life spans; they may have psychological trauma that affects their lives even today; and so forth.

Ladder Set B

B1. Answers will vary. Check students' answers for relevance and accuracy.

B2. Answers will vary based on the details on their list. Make sure students' categories make sense and are logically organized.

B3. Answers will vary. Generalizations should be broad, overarching statements about the differences between their lives as children today compared to life as a child during the Great Depression.

It's Electric!

Ladder Set B

B1. Answers will vary. Check students' list to ensure they include examples of the use of electricity only.

B2. Answers will vary. Students should group details into logical categories without using a miscellaneous or other category.

B3. Answers will vary. Generalizations should be broad, overarching statements about the use of electricity.

Ladder Set D

D1. Answers will vary. Students should restate the quotation in their own words and not merely make minor changes to the statement. For example, a possible response might be: "Electricity will be so common that only people who have time and money to waste will spend it on using candles."

D2. Answers will vary. Students should include the important elements of static electricity including charge build up, opposite charges attract, like charges repel, and overcharged objects will transfer charged particles to neutral objects.

D3. Answers will vary. Check students' answers for originality and audience appeal.

The Metric System vs. the U.S. Customary System

Ladder Set A

A1. *Metric system*: origin, goals, measurement of length, liquid, weight; prefixes; lack of conversion factors; time

U.S. Customary system: origin, the U.S. is the only country that hasn't converted; Omnibus Trade and Competitiveness Act of 1988; measurement of length, general volume, liquid volume, and weight; conversion factors; chart comparing conversion

A2. The French adopted the metric system because they wanted a standard, single unit to measure physical quantity without the need for conversion factors and with a common set of prefixes.

A3. Answers will vary. Possible answers may include: trade with foreign countries will become more difficult for the United States; the United States believes it does not have to conform to what the rest of the world is doing; the United States likes being different; it would be too difficult to change the entire nation to the metric system because most everyone learns the customary system in school, and so forth.

Ladder Set C

C1. Answers will vary. Students should clearly support the metric or the customary system. Check their answers for cohesion, logic, and supporting details.

C2. Answers will vary. Possible answers might include: The metric system is easier to convert between units; the customary system has units of measurement that are easier to pronounce and remember; the metric system is more organized and logical; the customary system has significantly different names for different measurement units that makes it less confusing.

C3. Answers will vary. Check students' answers for justification through relevant supporting details.